Faith & Sexuality
in the Church of Ireland

An EFIC publication

An EFIC publication

Evangelical Fellowship of Irish Clergy

www.efic.info

© EFIC committee

Published February 2012

Printed by www.lulu.com

ISBN 978-1-4716-1929-8

Abbreviations

ACoC	The Anglican Church of Canada
BCP	Book of Common Prayer
C of I	Church of Ireland
ECUSA	Episcopal Church USA (now TEC)
ESV	English Standard Version
LGBT	Lesbian, Gay, Bisexual, Transgender
NIV	New International Version
NLT	New Living Translation
NRSV	New Revised Standard Version
NT	The New Testament
OT	The Old Testament
TEC	The Episcopal Church (USA)

'If anyone loves me, he will obey my teaching. My Father will love him, and we will come to him and make our home with him.'

John 14:23

Contents

		Page
Introduction *Rev Trevor Johnston*		1

The current situation

1. Why not? We've changed our minds on slavery, women's ordination, divorce and ... *Rev Brian Courtney* — 6
2. Reflections of a serving clergyman. *Rev Neville Hughes* — 11
3. What is marriage? *Rev Tim Anderson* — 14
4. Isn't it simply in the genes? *Dermot O'Callaghan* — 17
5. Christian belief and sexuality – do two rights make a wrong? *Rev Barry Forde* — 21
6. Obsessed? The Anglican Communion and sex. *Rev Bill Atkins* — 30
7. What will be our witness to Ireland? *David Martin* — 35

The Biblical witness

8. "That's just your interpretation." *Rev Eddie Coulter* — 40
9. No longer relevant? What does the Old Testament say? *Rev William Press* — 44
10. Did Jesus have a view on same-sex unions? *Rev David Huss* — 49
11. In context. What does the (rest of the) New Testament say? *Rev Trevor Johnston* — 54

Pastoral relationships

12. The pastoral care of gay people and their families. *Rev David McClay* — 62
13. What example will we set our teens? *Johnny Beare* — 67
14. Listening to all sides – the witness of a celibate, homosexual Christian *Anonymous* — 71

Appendices

Further Reading — 76
The Kuala Lumpur Statement — 78
The Lambeth Conference 1998 Resolution I.10 — 80
The Jerusalem Declaration — 82

Introduction

Many of the contributors to this little volume never imagined themselves in print, including myself! But then again we never imagined that going into print on this issue would have been necessary. For nearly 2 millennia, the Church's approach to sexuality has remained unchanged and we had assumed that everyone thought the same things. That is: one woman and one man, in lifelong monogamy, ever since the Garden of Eden, an illustration of the greater relationship between Christ and his bride – the Church. Yet, for the first time in the Church of Ireland's history, the debate, which has raged across the Anglican Communion, is now on our own shores.

In the summer of 2011, a senior cleric entered a civil partnership in the full knowledge of his Bishop attracting the attention of many, lay and ordained. The media were interested and the 'factions' were either delighted or dismayed. This civil partnership was the confirmation of a 20-year-old same-gender relationship. Of course, cultural resistance to homosexuality is waning and the debate has moved from civil partnership to homosexual marriage. Sport, media, and parliament, to name but a few, have prominent homosexual people and society is mostly comfortable with the idea. Yet the Church is unsure. Age-old bonds of affection have been ruptured. Deeply held understandings have been questioned. Careless words have been shouted and much ink has been spilt in dealing with the matter.

So why has this issue got us so hot under the dog collar? Why human sexuality? Why has this roused such interest? Is it an unchecked homophobia (an irrational fear of homosexual people)? Is it a desire to suppress the civil rights of people and an opposition to justice and equality, regardless of sexual orientation? Is it a skewing of the Bible's message coupled with a warped interpretation which disregards or over-emphasises one aspect of a culturally and historically bound text, revealing our own prejudices?

Actually, it's none of the above. The Church is seeking to understand the complex issue of sexuality and to speak prophetically and lovingly with Biblical truth. Some might suggest that this is a distraction from the core work of preaching the Gospel, caring for and making disciples. Yet isn't God concerned with all aspects of our lives? He made us and made sex, therefore, he is deeply interested in the sex lives of his people. We are not irrationally frightened of homosexual people (the charge, if it's repeated and shouted loudly enough, might stick). Nor are we seeking to marginalise anyone, remove their rights or suppress them. We understand the position in law and support appropriate legal provision. It must be acknowledged that in addressing this, we are ourselves likely to become the marginalised in the world and, possibly, even the Church.

This issue has gotten us hot under the dog collar because we're deeply and passionately concerned about people and their inclusion - inclusion, that is, in the Kingdom of God. We are concerned that Christ's mind, already, univocally and clearly revealed in his Word will not be followed or obeyed. We are compassionately concerned about humanity, which, as Romans 1 puts it, has suppressed the obvious truth about God in its desire to worship created things rather than the Creator. We are compassionately concerned about the inclusion of all people in the Kingdom of God. We rejoice in the Gospel that speaks of forgiveness, new hope and eternal life. However, we are acutely aware that God excludes those who are unrepentant, persistent and deliberate.

Society doesn't allow for the "that is what some of you were" (1 Corinthians 6:11). It doesn't allow for sin to become a past tense, or for the possibility of forgiveness and the inclusion of those who were once active in various sins. The fear of the contributors to this book is that the Church will follow suit and distort the Gospel of inclusion in the Kingdom of God. This inclusion has been achieved through the death of Christ for our sins, a faith and repentance that renounces the things for which Christ died, and a turning away from them by the grace of God, these being the only appropriate responses. This is difficult and uncomfortable territory. Issues such as sex and sexuality are not usual talking points for we who are predominantly from an admittedly conservative culture.

The Church of Ireland is amongst the last of the major Western Anglican provinces to deal with this issue. We observe North American brothers and sisters being pilloried in the law courts and removed from their church buildings because of this issue. Even a world-renowned theologian of the stature of the Rev Canon Dr JI Packer has lost his licence to officiate and a new Anglican entity has been formed in North America. Incidentally, Dr Packer has described this crisis as of the same importance as the Arian controversy in the fourth century.

We watch the worldwide Anglican Communion rip itself apart as a decades-long game of stealth and gradual change is played. Process has superseded Gospel; words, discussions, and endless meetings have taken over from the Gospel word and the 'faith once delivered'. We know the contradictions within the Church of England and are aware of friends in the Church of Scotland. The trickle of ministerial resignations (now congregations) from that denomination is growing into a fast flowing river. All conducted in a time when society is pluralistic, relativistic and uncertain as to the meaning of words and their place. All conducted in a time when the Gospel word must be shared and grow, because Christ is soon returning and eternity is real.

Thus, the contributors have put pen to paper, or finger to keyboard, to contribute to the debate. We have deliberately sought to draw on the ordinary experience and expertise of ordinary clergy and lay people. We have sought to address the ordinary person in the typical pew of a typical parish in the Church of Ireland. We pray that the reader will find our faltering words on faith and sexuality in the Church of Ireland helpful. Moreover, we pray that the reader will join with us in praying for our Church as she seeks to continue to love and serve her Lord at this crucial time in her history.

Rev Trevor Johnston
EFIC chairperson

The Current Situation

1

Why not? We've changed our minds on slavery, women's ordination, divorce and . . .

Rev Canon Brian Courtney was, until his retirement, the Rector of Enniskillen and a long-standing member of General Synod.

It is always alarming and sad when Christians are open to the accusation of picking and choosing which Scripture to apply and which to ignore. So when some opposing the orthodox view that homosexual practice is a sin suggest that traditionalists are inconsistent in applying Scripture they are entitled to a response.

The charge is straightforward: the critics imply there was a time when evangelical and traditional Christians used the Bible to justify slavery and condemn divorce and women's ordination. Now the same people reject slavery and accept divorce and female ordination - and claim biblical support!

Slavery
There is no question but that in different times and places Christians accepted slavery as part of the social norm. Had we lived in certain cultures there is nothing to say we would have been moved to challenge the standards of our times. Among those who did were the Christians of the Clapham Sect and most notably, William Wilberforce.

William J. Webb[1] argues that in some areas of human behaviour,

Scripture offers what we could think of as 'an evolving ethic'. Applying this to slaves he suggests that in the earlier books of the OT there is an acceptance of the practice of slavery which had built-in protection for slaves, something which would not have been the case in contemporary cultures. This situation progresses until we meet Paul's statement that 'there is no longer Jew or Greek, there is no longer slave or free, there is no longer male and female; for all of you are one in Christ Jesus' (Galatians 3:28).

Gordon Wenham points out that slavery in ancient Israel is not to be confused with slavery as we think of it in more modern times[2]. Israelites generally lived off the land and if crops failed and hardship came then one means of survival was to be indentured into the household of a more wealthy relative or neighbour. The 'slave' worked for his or her keep and in return was housed and fed and be freed after six years of service (Exodus 21:2). Within Israel 'slavery' was a means whereby those in need could receive support when facing adverse circumstances.

The OT also refers to people from other cultures who are slaves to Israelites and these foreign slaves do not enjoy the same privileges given to Israelite slaves. Commenting on this Richard Hess identifies at least two qualifications: 'First . . . the prohibition against placing marks on the body contradicts the requirement that all permanent slaves be so marked (Exodus 21:6; Deuteronomy 15:17) and renders slaveholding impossible for Israelites. Full obedience of the Levitical law will pull away from the practice of keeping slaves. Second, Christians must understand that the picture in the NT is one in which the barriers between nations have been broken down (Ephesians 2:11-22) and the traditional distinctions of status have been nullified (Galatians 3:28). Thus, the process by which the vestiges of slavery became abolished were initiated in the OT and achieved their full flowering in the NT[3].

Divorce
When we Church of Ireland folk think of changing our minds on divorce we need to recognise that what has changed is the General

Synod's ruling in 1996 to permit the remarriage of divorced persons in church.

Since the Reformation there have been different approaches to divorce within Protestantism. Practically this means that in Ireland our Methodist and Presbyterian neighbours have had procedures for marrying the divorced long before we Anglicans did.

Within the Church of Ireland those clergy who do not wish to participate by officiating in the marriage of a person with a living but divorced spouse are not required to do so and each diocese makes provision for clergy to 'opt out'. In Scripture divorce, while never the ideal, is seen as a concession to the fallen state of humanity.

Women's Ordination
While Anglicanism has a developed structure of ministry and church order, we must concede that others claim NT authority for their different ministry models, hence Presbyterianism and Congregationalism. Even within Anglicanism there are differing understandings of ordination and of the ordination of women which some faithful Anglicans, both Anglo-catholic and Reformed, reject as unscriptural.

Some parts of the Anglican Communion where women are ordained have legislation that allows those who in conscience cannot accept this form of ministry to distance themselves from direct involvement with it. Scripture tells us much about the servant nature of ministry yet we could often wish, humanly speaking, that it was even more explicit.

Homosexuality
With the issue of slavery there is a perceived development throughout Scripture; both sides of the debate over divorce can be traced back to bible times; regarding the ordination of women there are wider and related issues concerning our understanding of the nature of male and female calling and also our view of ordination itself.

When we turn to Scripture's pronouncements on homosexuality there is no evidence of a developing ethic, differing strands of approach, vagueness or silence. Just as is the case with adultery, homosexual sex is uniformly and unequivocally condemned. There is no equivocation and there are no exceptions whether our source is the Pentateuch or the epistles, the verdict is the same, as an examination of the various relevant passages indicate.

Just as significant is the blueprint for living found in the Creation accounts in Genesis. We are made, male and female, in the image of God and given the command to 'Be fruitful and multiply and fill the earth' (Genesis 1:28). In Matthew 19 our Lord repeats and so endorses this Creation ordinance that God intends that natural bodily union is to be between male and female.

It is worth underlining Webb's conclusion that with regard to sexual morality there is no movement within the Bible departing from the Levitical prohibitions on adultery, homosexual activity, incest and bestiality[4]. The NT clearly endorses the teaching of Leviticus 18:22 and 20:13 (Romans 1:26-27; 1 Corinthians 6:9-11; 1 Timothy 1:10). It is also significant that over a relatively short period of time we see Paul, with his strict Jewish background, setting aside what he had been taught from youth regarding food laws and sacrifices, circumcision and ritual, but upholding orthodox Hebrew teaching on sexual behaviour. When we take or leave oysters and the wearing of tweed and adhere to Levitical teaching on sexuality we are merely following in the footsteps of the Apostle and keeping in step with God's purposes in Creation.

Should you or I find our long-held beliefs and lifestyle at odds with the Word of God then we must be ready to change our minds. To date, the gay lobby has failed to demonstrate that homosexual sex is consistent with biblical faith.

[1] *Slaves, Women & Homosexuals*, IVP, 2001
[2] *Leviticus*, NICOT, Eerdmans, p322f

[3] *Leviticus*, (EBC, Zondervan, Revised Edition, 2008, 1979) p808f
[4] Ibid.

2
Reflections of a serving clergyman

My name is Neville Hughes. Most probably we have never met and I would like to thank you for taking a few moments to read my comments. I have been Church of Ireland all my life – born, 'bred and buttered' C of I. I am married to Maureen and we have been blessed with three daughters – all of whom have given me great support over the years.

By way of background, I was commissioned as a Diocesan Lay Reader in Armagh Diocese in 1980 and on 30th June 1991 I was ordained. I have been serving as the Rector of the Mullabrack and Kilcluney parishes in the Diocese of Armagh since May 2000.

Before entering the Ordained Ministry I was employed for a number of years as a Regional Programme Manager with a very large Housing Authority in Northern Ireland.

Like a great many people, both ordained and lay, I have been greatly saddened and concerned about the current crisis in which, as members of the Church of Ireland, we find ourselves. I reflect upon my ordination and the vows I took at that time. I sincerely and formally promised 'to exercise (my) ministry duly, to the honour of God and the edifying of his Church'. I cannot help but wonder, does a homosexual lifestyle, or a clergyman's same-sex partnership, honour God and edify his Church?

I remember the Archbishop asking me, 'Do you trust that you are inwardly moved by the Holy Spirit ... to serve God for the promoting of his glory and the edifying of his people?' I took seriously the very searching question, 'Do you unfeignedly believe all the Canonical Scriptures of the Old and New Testament?' By extension this includes the Bible's teaching on homosexuality and its prohibitions on same-sex relationships. I remember reading over the service and remarking to myself that the vows to be taken had direct implications not only for me but also for my family: 'will you apply all your diligence to frame and fashion your own lives and the lives of your families, according to the Doctrine of Christ; and to make both yourselves and them, as much as in you lieth, wholesome examples of the flock of Christ?' This is a direct call to holiness of life and to be a good example to the parishioners entrusted to my care.

I cannot help but think of those promises when I consider the crisis we are now facing. I still feel the weight of that moment when the Archbishop placed a copy of the New Testament in my hands and directed me with the words 'Take thou authority to read … to preach … .' As a minister within our Church, this is where I derive my authority; this is my rule; this is my guide. And so I approach the current crisis reflecting upon the words of my ordination and the vows I took.

I also reflect upon the words of St Paul in the NT, which are pertinent to all serving clergymen. He instructed his young assistant Timothy to 'watch your life and doctrine closely' (1 Timothy 4:16). St Paul goes on to say, 'A deacon must be the husband of but one wife and must manage his household well' (1 Timothy 3:12). And in 2 Timothy 4:2 St Paul instructs Timothy to 'Preach the Word … correct rebuke and encourage with great patience and careful instruction.'

All this floods into my mind when I try to reconcile the current crisis we are in with the vows all of us clergy have taken. Our ordination vows and promises have always been based upon the Word of God. These are the things we have subscribed to, before God, at our ordinations.

While no doubt some are more inclined to homosexual desires, I believe its practice is a lifestyle choice. I cannot approve or condone such a choice, but I respect the right of the individual to make that choice. My grave concern in the current crisis is with clergy in leadership roles within the Church. Is our Church being too anxious to be 'inclusive'? Will it approve a form of words which, in themselves, will be so vague as to mean nothing? Will it thereby promote homosexuality as a legitimate lifestyle choice fitting for members of the clergy while, in some contrived way, still in keeping with Scripture? This would be very distressing. How can General Synod honestly square this circle? Should we not as serving clergy be asked to remain faithful to our vows, faithful to the teaching of Scripture and faithful to the flock we have been called to serve?

I leave the final few words to St Paul: 'For the time will come when men will not put up with sound doctrine. Instead, to suit their own desires, they will gather around them a great number of teachers to say what their itching ears want to hear. They will turn their ears away from the truth and turn aside to myths. But you, keep your head in all situations, endure hardship, do the work of an evangelist, discharge all the duties of your ministry.' (2 Timothy 4:3-5).

3
What is marriage?

Rev Tim Anderson is the Rector of St Elizabeth's Parish Church, Dundonald, Belfast and a graduate in Theology of the University of Oxford.

A Christian discussion of marriage and human sexuality has to begin with the opening pages of the Bible. When Jesus was asked about these issues he pointed to God's created intention (Matthew 19:4-6) and the apostle Paul did the same (Ephesians 5:31-32). The passage we will look at therefore, is Genesis 2:18-25. There is so much to be said from these verses, but a couple of things will suffice.

First, *the Lord's perfect provision.* Verses 21-23: 'So the Lord God caused the man to fall into a deep sleep; and while he was sleeping, he took one of the man's ribs and closed up the place with flesh. Then the Lord God made a woman from the rib He had taken out of man, and He brought her to the man. The man said, "This is now bone of my bones and flesh of my flesh; she shall be called 'woman', for she was taken out of man."'

Adam recognises the woman to be an exact match for his need. She is made by God out of the rib of Adam, and is brought by God to Adam to be united to him. Adam looks at the woman; and he simply gasps with delight—'This is now bone of my bones.'

This unique match is expressed in a couple of ways. First, in the way she is made. She was not made from the dust of the ground like man was made. Instead the Lord made her from man. Verse 22: 'The Lord God made a woman from the rib.' God's perfect design goes in two directions. On the one hand man should find his completeness in woman. Equally however, God's perfect design is also that woman, to find her completeness, must come home to man - to where she belongs. To find her completeness, she must return to him and to no other. Man and woman, therefore, are an exact match for each other.

The second way this unique match between the man and woman is expressed is in the name the woman was given. We see from verse 23 that Adam was the one who named the woman. Adam says: 'She shall be called woman for she was taken out of man.' Adam names the woman. Yet in doing so he was not taking upon himself that same authority by which he named the animals. He does indeed have authority and headship over the woman in so far as he was the first of the two to be created. Nevertheless, in naming the woman, Adam was not subordinating her to his rule and dominion. Instead he is recognising and acknowledging what she is in herself. She is the one who is taken out of man that she may complement him in his work: the exact match.

Now the problem is that the Fall of man (mankind's rebellion to God and His way) has twisted and warped this perfect design. The formal acceptance of civil partnerships as an alternative union alongside traditional marriage is an example of this. The original purpose of the Civil Partnerships Act in 2004 was to provide a scheme that would give legal recognition to homosexual relationships. A civil partnership is a relationship between two people of the same sex formed when they register as civil partners of each other. This partnership ends only on death, dissolution or annulment. In effect therefore, a civil partnership is a 'gay marriage' in all but name (i.e. a physical, social and emotional union). However, such a 'union' is vastly different from God's perfect union in heterosexual marriage - and the ultimate proof of this is its complete inability to lead to the procreation of children.

So first, a perfect provision. Second, *a lasting principle*. Verses 24 and 25: 'For this reason a man will leave his father and mother and be united to his wife, and they will become one flesh. The man and his wife were both naked, and they felt no shame.' Due to the Lord's provision of a woman to help the man in his isolation, the two become one flesh. That is how perfect and complete this design of God is. One plus one equals one! When a man leaves his father and mother to be joined to his wife they become together a new unit (physically, socially, emotionally, and in Christ, spiritually). Indeed this union is so strong, so positive, so perfect, that it is a permanent condition. It is a life-long state. Till death us do part. Notice also in verse 24 that the man is united and joined to his wife, not his wives. So not only is this union a permanent one it is also an exclusive union between one man and one woman.

This is why sex outside of marriage, whether heterosexual or homosexual, is an offence to our creator God. It is a complete breakdown of any kind of commitment or cleaving. Fornication (sex before marriage) and adultery (sex within marriage with someone who is not your spouse), no matter how stable a relationship may be, is sin and grieves God. Yes, sex is a good gift of God. Yet when it used wrongly, it strikes at the very heart of God's purposes for the deepest of all human relationships.

This then is the nature of human sexuality in general and marriage in particular. It is a wonderful gift from God, and a gift that is as old as creation itself. It is not a social institution that will pass away with time. Nor is it merely a private arrangement between two people no matter what their gender. Neither should the definition of marriage be broadened to include a same sex union (which is the purpose of a civil partnership). Marriage is a permanent part of God's created order: an exclusive, physical union between one man and one woman. Let us thank God for this and do all that we can in church and society to promote his will by our witness and example.

4

Isn't it simply in the genes?

Dermot O'Callaghan is a lay reader in the diocese of Down and Dromore and a member of General Synod.

I used to think that people who identified as gay were 'born that way'. It was comparable to the colour of one's skin or being left-handed – God had made them that way. It seemed obvious – you could recognise them not just by their mannerisms (at least in the case of men) but often from their physical appearance. But now I have met so many gay men and lesbians whom I could not distinguish in any way from heterosexuals, that I have had to revise my opinion about recognising them. I have also come to a different view as to the causes of same-sex attraction.

The reader might assume that if I don't think that homosexuality is usually innate (inborn) then I must think that people have deliberately chosen to be that way, but when gay people tell me that they did not choose their feelings any more than I chose my heterosexual feelings, I believe them. So what causes same-sex attraction if it is not primarily genes or choice?

Recent Scientific Research

Let's look at a brief history of scientific research over the past forty years. In the 1970s most scientists assumed that homosexuality had a psychosocial cause – something to do with psychology or sociology in a person's life experience or 'environment'. But when in 1981 a landmark study[1] failed to find the expected single experiential pathway to homosexuality, the focus switched to looking for biological causes – a switch from nurture to nature. Since then, biological theories – 'gay gene', 'gay brain', mother-to-baby hormonal transfers and many others – have been exhaustively researched, but with little result.

An important tool has been twin studies, which help to differentiate between nature and nurture. If homosexuality is 'in the genes', then if one identical twin is gay, the co-twin should always be gay too. Although early twin studies seemed to point in that direction, an important study in 2000 by Michael Bailey found that for 27 pairs of identical twins of whom one was gay, in only 3 cases was the other also gay – a 'pairwise concordance' of just 11%[2]. Bailey said his study 'did not provide statistically significant support for the importance of genetic factors for sexual orientation.'

Similarly, Francis Collins, who directed the Human Genome Project (which found no 'gay gene') considers that the heritability of homosexuality may be less than 20%.

Pointers towards nurture causes
After thirty years of searching for biological causes, it seems reasonable to look again at possible psychosocial explanations. Several interesting studies offer a way forward. A widely respected study led by Edward Laumann, *The Social Organization of Sexuality*,[3] says (p307) that a pattern of homosexuality similar to those of biologically-based traits such as left-handedness or intelligence is 'exactly what we do not find.' Also, in discussing male homosexuality, it says (p309) that the theory that 'the environment in which people grow up affects their sexuality in very basic ways' is 'exactly one way to read many of the patterns that we have found.' Laumann found that women who received higher education were more likely to identify as lesbians. Also, both males and females who experienced same-sex attraction were much more likely than others to have experienced childhood sexual abuse (*though most gay people were not abused*). These are environmental factors.

Lisa Diamond tracked a group of non-heterosexual women over a decade and found considerable 'fluidity' of sexuality over time. Their sexual orientation changed – it was not genetically fixed[4].

A study by Savin-Williams and Ream[5] found that more than half of those who experience same-sex attraction at age 16 no longer do so at age 17. It would thus be irresponsible to counsel affirmation of same-sex feelings in an adolescent on the grounds that the feelings are intrinsic and the child is therefore homosexual.

A Danish study entitled *Childhood Family Correlates of Heterosexual and Homosexual Marriages* (same-sex marriage is available in Denmark)[6] said, 'Our study provides population-based, prospective evidence that childhood family experiences are important determinants of heterosexual and homosexual marriage decisions in adulthood.' This is an extraordinary claim – that a person's childhood experiences can be so strong as to influence whether in adult life he/ she will marry a man or a woman. The study identified some underlying factors, including such things as parental divorce or death of a parent.

All studies have some methodological weaknesses, so it would be wise not to be too prescriptive as to precise causes. But it seems that people are not usually 'born gay'. A better understanding of the factors involved should emerge during the next decade if the research focus switches back from biology to life experience.

Conclusion

So do genes do nothing? Well, a genetic contribution of 10% - 20% is a very weak influence – not enough to predetermine a person's sexuality.

Two consequences arise from this discussion. First, if homosexuality is caused largely by environmental factors, it may be possible that other (counter-acting) environmental factors could reverse the process (though it should not be assumed that environmental causes are easier to change than biological ones, and no exaggerated claims should be made as to likely outcomes)[7]. Such a course of action should be undertaken only at the voluntary request of the person concerned, without coercion from family or church. But people should not be put off by fears of 'harm' from seeking responsibly conducted counselling[8]. The 'friendly' counselling approaches of today are very different from the 'Frankenstein' methods of the 1960's.

Secondly, if people are not born gay, they are born heterosexual and any efforts that they make to move away from unwanted same-sex attraction are not a *violation* of their God-given sexuality, but a *return* to it.

Finally, this is not about 'blaming' either the parents or the child. Research appears to show that causal factors for same-sex attraction will more commonly be found in aspects of early life experience that are painful for the individual but are neither freely chosen nor an indication of bad parenting.

[1] Bell, A.P., Weinberg, M.S. & Hammersmith, S.K. *Sexual preference: Its development in men and women.* (Bloomington, IN: Indiana University Press, 1981).
[2] This 11% figure was reported in the study as 20% because it was considered statistically appropriate to double count the twin pairs where both were gay. This procedure is explained in detail in a very useful book, S Jones & M Yarhouse *Homosexuality: The Use of Scientific Research in the Church's Moral Debate*, (Leicester: IVP, 2000) pp 75-77.
[3] E O Laumann et al *The Social Organization of Sexuality*, (University of Chicago Press, 1994)
[4] L Diamond *Female Bisexuality From Adolescence to Adulthood: Results From a 10-Year Longitudinal Study*, (Development Psychology 2008, 44:1) pp 5-14.
[5] Savin-Williams, R.C. and Ream, G.L *Prevalence and Stability of Sexual Orientation Components During Adolescence and Young Adulthood*, Archives of Sexual Behaviour 36, 2007 pp385-394. This is helpfully analysed by Dr Neil Whitehead at http://www.mygenes.co.nz/Change.htm
[6] M Frisch, A Hviid *Childhood Correlates of Heterosexual and Homosexual Marriages: A National Cohort Study of Two Million Danes*, (Archives of Sexual Behaviour 35:5, Oct 2006) pp 533-547.
[7] The Christian Medical Fellowship has produced a helpful booklet on this subject: A Goddard, G Harrison *Unwanted Same-Sex Attraction – Issues of pastoral counselling and support* (Christian Medical Fellowship 2011) www.cmf.org.uk
[8] See S Jones & M Yarhouse *Ex Gays? An Extended Longitudinal Study of Attempted Religiously Mediated Change in Sexual Orientation* http://wthrockmorton.com/wp-content/uploads/2009/08/Jones-and-Yarhouse-Final.pdf

5

Christian Belief and Sexuality - do two rights make a wrong?

A former barrister, the Rev Barry Forde is the Church of Ireland chaplain to Queens University, Belfast.

The 'Clearing the Ground' inquiry, led by the All-Party Parliamentary Group, Christians in Parliament, has been seeking to establish whether law and public policy are having an adverse impact on Christian freedoms in the UK[1]. In December 2011 the former Archbishop of Canterbury, Lord Carey, heavily criticised the British Government for not backing four British Christians who are taking cases to the European Court of Human Rights. Two of the four cases involve wearing symbols at the workplace, the other two relate to how the freedom of Christians to act in accordance with their conscience has been trumped by homosexual rights. This failure, according to Lord Carey, is the 'result of a liberal establishment that has become deeply illiberal'[2].

In Northern Ireland the recent Bill of Rights proposals sought to affirm the right to religious belief and practice. However, unlike other rights this right was made subject to explicitly stated limitations 'necessary in a democratic society in the interests of public safety, for the protection of public order, health or morals, or for the protection of the rights and freedom of others'.[3] In the same proposals it is proposed that 'no one shall be unfairly discriminated against by any public authority on any ground such as....religion or belief, sexual orientation'[4] . This immediately begs the question - when is it fair to discriminate? In many areas, including the right not to be discriminated against on the grounds of sexual orientation, this is not even considered. The right to religious belief can however, be fairly discriminated against according to the needs of democratic society (which could, in all logic, vote for the abolition of religion), be ranked second to undefined yet assumed 'public morals', and be a lesser weight when competing with the rights of others. It is a proposed right, but is it a marginalised one?

In the Republic of Ireland the role of the Church and its relationship to the State has come under the closest scrutiny in modern times. For obvious and tragic reasons the ongoing inquiries into child abuse scandals has left many with a deep distrust of the dominant Catholic church. When the Taoiseach, Enda Kenny made 'that speech' in the Dail on the Cloyne report it was reported as a watershed moment for a Government in Ireland who would be adopting a less 'deferential attitude to the Vatican and the Catholic church'[5].

Many Christians are nervous. The law of the land is changing. The consensus of the nation can no longer be broadly aligned with traditional Christian beliefs, morals or values. Human rights, it seems, protect everyone except those who hold to traditional Christian beliefs, or at least until they wish to live out their lives as if their beliefs actually mean something. There is a fear attached to being a Christian in the workplace, to what our children get taught in schools, to the unseen but forceful tides of culture that seem to drag us ever further away from safer shores. Other Christians are processing. Rather than possessing an instinctive fear of such changes they want to know how we can jump in and swim. Times change, and so how can we move with the times. They want to know how can we be relevant if we live in the past? How can we embrace these new found social values of openness, tolerance, and freedom, and are these not the values of the gospel anyway?

How are we to proceed from here? It will be impossible to think upon such huge topics as human rights, or the relationship between church and state, in such a short space. But there are a number of things that can be said.

The Right language is God's language
First, we need <u>not be afraid</u>. Article 1 of the Universal Declaration of Human Rights is bold and unequivocal:

All human beings are born free and equal in dignity and rights. They are endowed with reason and conscience and should act towards one another in a spirit of brotherhood.

Signed in 1948 this Declaration was humanity's *'Never Again'* to the atrocities of the Second World War. Affirming the dignity and status of all human beings, it also expresses the privilege we have of exercising both reason and conscience, and affirms our responsibility to live in community with one another. Christians recognise such foundational and universal language. Christian belief asserts that, from the foundation of the world that we are created in the image and likeness of God. We have dignity, status. We are not here by chance, an accident, an afterthought, the result of a squabble between rivalling deities (as in ancient thought), nor a mere by-product of time, chance and the right concoction of liquids, mass and gasses (in certain modern scientific thinking). In God's creative act He bestowed upon us the privilege of understanding His will, the source of our reason and conscience, and in His will gave us the gift of community. The only thing not good in all of creation was isolation. The Triune God, who lives in intimate fellowship and community as Father, Son, and Holy Spirit, saw that we would indeed image His likeness by living in community with one another. We further image His likeness by undertaking our responsibility to represent God and the goodness of God towards one another and the whole created order. The creator grants us dominion over the earth that we might care for it as He does. He who breathed life into man fashioned woman out of man so that together they could enjoin with God in the joy of creating a boy who would be 'the image of his dad', a girl who is 'just like her mother'.

Dignity. Identity. Reason. Freedom. Responsibility. Community. Relationships. These are the foundational promises of Genesis. They are worked out on the pages of scripture as kingdom values. The language of rights is our language (or better put, it is God's language). Christians need have no fear of human rights as a concept, just the 'human' bit.

It's the 'human' bit that's not right
Christians speak of universal sin, and then act like everyone else is wrong. We, as Christian people, desperately need to show <u>Honest Humility</u>. Universal Human Rights were not established in 1948, just

declared in a form that has been pivotal in shaping the second half on the 20th and the early part of the 21st century. But rights, and the failure of human beings to live up to the dignity, status and responsibility that we understand to be gifts of God, have been claimed and violated from time immemorial. The trouble is, in western history, the church institutionally has leaned more favourably towards the violation end of the spectrum, even if a few conscientious objectors fought the good fight, no matter what. The Irish penal laws, the slave trade, racial segregation in the US, apartheid in South Africa, the treatment of women as second class citizens, have all been reasons for shame for the church at some time or in some place. The list goes on and, in the current debate, the attitude of the church towards same-sex relationships is usually added as yet another example of how the church cannot be trusted to get it right. But let's not just throw stones at ivory towers and faceless institutions. Do I afford to all others the dignity and status they deserve as being created by Almighty God? Do I align my reason and conscience in harmony with the Father's will? Do I exercise care and stewardship towards the world around me? Do I live without fault in my relationships, society and culture? The answer for me, is no. The problem of upholding human rights has, more often than not, been with the being human part of the equation. We get it wrong. God bestowed upon us rights and responsibilities, and we have constantly come up short.

Should we be indignant then when, upon examination of the modern and often secular human rights purposes, goals and agenda, we find that here too human beings come up short? If, as Christians, we have had the sure foundation and we still managed to build bad houses and distorted empires, can we be dismissive of the world's attempts to do any better? No, we should not. We should first exercise humility, realising that far too often we kicked and missed. But this does not mean that we only ever kick and miss or that now we may simply be kicked. We will have issues with human rights when they are founded on modern secular philosophy. We will question the priority given to some rights, including those on sexual orientation, over those of religious belief, freedom and conscience. We will query the individualism that now permeates modern rights. We should highlight the manner in which conflicting rights set individuals and communities in direct opposition to one another. It is right that we do so. However, humility acknowledges that the church has, in the past, been guilty of creating a world in its own image, rather than being a people in the world who reflect God's image. The world is changing and we who have much reason to repent of our past need to exercise caution before we become too strident in the present.

Can things be made right?

We need to face up to some pretty complex cultural realities. As we do we need to realise that Christians will respond to these realities in differing ways. There is no perfect response, only prayerfully considered ones as issue by issue, person by person, story by story, we attempt to be instruments of healing and love and direction (and indeed to receive all three) in a broken world. In a world that does not seek to govern on the basis of Christian doctrine however we will need to hold in tension what we believe to be right, to consider what it is realistic to expect within our culture, and what it might be possible to achieve. What follows are some very tentative suggestions as to what this *may* look like in practice.

First, human rights seek to provide a framework within which all can live fairly. We should acknowledge the goodness in this aspiration, whilst maintaining the Christian position that the rights of this world will not ultimately put this world to rights. We must continue, through considered and constant biblical and theological reflection, to affirm the central core values of who we are in Christ. This is important because of the false line of reasoning that asserts, 'because x is a human right, the church should adhere to it'. The church, however, should be affirming that our rights are not founded simply on being human, but rather on the God who made us a human being. We should hold fast to our fundamental convictions about what is right, biblically and theologically, in relation to human sexuality. We should, however, be slow to think or suggest that if only the world was governed by us that somehow we would get it right. That somehow we have a model that we are capable of working. Our models are not the point. Staying faithful no matter what the model, that is the point. This does not mean that we go looking for conflict, perversely thinking that if the world is against us then God is on our side. Rather, it means that we seek to be on God's side. That we image the likeness of the King, seeking that His will be done.

Second, we must be realistic about the culture in which we live. Jesus said that we render under Caesar what is Caesar's and unto God what is God, knowing full well that all civic rulers and authorities are under God and so, the irony goes, therefore so too is Caesar. He died under the authority of Pilate, reminding Pilate along the way that the only authority he had came from God. Though they never knew it, Jesus was telling both them and us what is theologically right. God is in control. Yet, in the realism of everyday life taxes were still paid, and according to the limited possibilities of Roman law, death still ensued. God, remember, remained in control. There are many aspects of civic life that we may struggle with, and on some we are right to raise an objection. We may believe that same-sex relationships are not within the will of God, but if the politics of our day seeks to provide those in such relationships with the same status, tax-breaks, pension and inheritance rights as those in heterosexual marriages, then what are we to do - withdraw from society, picket the pension companies, protest to the tax authorities? Of course not. We do not stop banking because we disagree with how the government oversees financial regulation. We do not seek for blasphemy to be made a criminal offence even though we find it offensive. There are lots of differing aspects of life and of governance with which we may uncomfortable, but we live in this world and should continually seek, in love, to seek the good of the city even when we can be quite clear that there are issues on which we disagree.

Being realistic does not mean being defeatist. Not all rights can be equal because rights conflict and something has to give. Rights are hierarchical, and the right to religious freedom is pretty near the bottom of the food chain. There are many questions that can be asked.

- It is imperative that we question the basis on which rights are determined. How are they arrived at? A governmental think-tank, a lobby group of interested parties, a democratic vote, the interests of the majority, the need to protect a minority, the work of human rights specialists, or all of the above? Probably the latter, reflecting different needs and concerns and circumstances. The point is not to say that these mechanisms for arriving at a right are necessarily wrong. It is to question the presumption that good governance is better than God governance. That decisions on morality and ethics might be taken without recourse to the life and teaching of the church and that somehow, once established, such rights will necessarily lead to a better society for all.

- We can query why the right to religious belief is made subject to other rights. We can question the Bill of Rights proposals and the discrimination against religious rights in favour of democracy, public health or morals, the rights of others. Discrimination works in many directions and it may not be too long before Christians begin to understand the hurt and injustice that comes with being a minority.

- We can continue to support the right of Christian organisations and individuals to act in accordance with their beliefs and consciences, free of accusatory claims of being prejudiced or suffering from some sort of phobia. We can highlight that in fact one right is being preferred over another. We can question why this is so.

These are good questions because they shift the conversation away from our being fearful and in retreat towards a dialogue conducted on equal footing. Suddenly everyone is engaged in the issue of why they think what they think. Christians need to be ready to do the same.

Being realistic also means being patient. Patient both with those who proclaim rights and those who claim rights with which we are in disagreement. The journey from who we are to who God wants us to be is a lifelong one for each of us. We should allow time for individuals to process how standing on the protection afforded by rights is less of a sure foundation than surrendering to the will and promises of God. Being patient recognises that we all fall short, but it does not have to affirm any of our shortcomings by creating a legislative or liturgical space within the life and teaching of the church. Being patient means we may have to allow time for society to realise the futility of trying to govern itself to the exclusion of God, but that does not mean we cannot speak up for the implementation of kingdom values within the public square now.

Third, what might it be possible to achieve? Enter the minefield! Perhaps, it is simply the case that as we emerge from a long period of time in history when the church had a huge say in public life, people just do not wish to hear it anymore. If this is the case then we shall be in no different a place from the people of God as we meet them on the pages of scripture and across history, time and place. A great number lived, and continue to live, in cultures in which Christian doctrine is not the basis for organising civic life. Much of the biblical narrative is focussed on being outside of the garden, or the promised land. Even when the reins of the promised land or Christendom were taken under control can we really say that those who proclaimed to be God's people represented Him truly in the world? There has rarely been a time when God's people have had it all their own way - politically, morally, ethically, worshipfully. In those brief moments when they have tried that 'human bit' kept getting in the way. We should not be surprised therefore when, as Christian people, we find ourselves living in the face of conflicting views, values, political ideologies, and social rules. If this brings favour, prosperity, respect and the good of the city then we will be in a long line of biblical characters who sought to do the same in their own era. If this brings cursing, labelling, despising, and the forceful imposition of the city upon us, then we will be in a long line of biblical characters who faced exactly the same (sometimes the same characters, as on some issues they were able to work with the world around them, and on others they could not acquiesce).

This is not to be flippant with our role in society or the reputation of the church. We are to be a people who bring God's blessing to the nations, who seek out followers of Christ. The church that simply objects is unlikely to mediate God's favour to the world. The church that simply acquiesces is equally unlikely to represent God's kingdom in the world. The question of the sort of world we want to live in, the type of society we wish to share in, is, for Christian believers, a Kingdom question. It is a question about a world lived under the rule of God and enjoying His blessing. The conversation for Christians is about more than just living with rights that protect equal and opposite parties and individuals. It is about God's peace, God's wholeness, God's Shalom. We know we are not there yet, but in every conversation, action, question, moment of protest, time of regress, we must look to be signposts to the Kingdom of God. It's the right thing to do.

[1]http://www.christiantoday.com/article/parliamentary.inquiry.to.review.freedoms. for.christians/28491.htm

[2] http://www.christianconcern.com/our-concerns/religious-freedom/government-under-fire-from-former-archbishop-of-canterbury

[3] NIHRC, *A Bill of Rights for Northern Ireland - Advice to the Secretary of the State"*, 10 December 2008,
http://www.nihrc.org/dms/data/NIHRC/attachments/dd/files/51/A_Bill_of_Rights_for_Northern_Ireland_%28December_2008%29.pdf, p. 29

[4] Ibid, p. 33

[5] Irish Times, July 23, 2011. Noel Whelan,
http://www.irishtimes.com/newspaper/opinion/2011/0723/1224301201157.html?via=rel

6
Obsessed?
The Anglican Communion and Sex.

A former missionary in the Middle East, the Rev Bill Atkins is the Rector of the South Leitrim group of parishes.

It is sometimes claimed that Anglican churches are strong on tradition and weak on doctrine, that we have an organisational and institutional unity, but limitless variety and toleration for a diversity of viewpoints. Bishop Stephen Neill in his Book 'Anglicanism' wrote,

> *'What are the special theological doctrines of the Church of England and the Anglican churches in fellowship with it? The answer is that there are no special Anglican theological doctrines, there is no particular Anglican theology.'[1]*

There may be no *special* Anglican doctrines, but this simply means that Anglican doctrine is the 'doctrine of the Scriptures and such of the Fathers as are agreeable to the Scriptures'[2]. In other words, we believe Christian doctrines taken from the Bible, nothing more and nothing less. This is why we call ourselves the Church of Ireland. We hold to the Catholic faith, in continuity with the primitive church and the apostles, via the English reformation which was itself a return to our apostolic and Biblical roots. I believe that it is faithfulness to this tradition that could lead to Christian unity in these islands.

However, there is a danger that we could become a mere sect, abandoning apostolic doctrine and discipline and capitulating to the spirit of the age. One of our bishops has stated at Synod that homosexuality is not divisive and that you can have alternative viewpoints in one church. Actually, the issue of homosexuality has torn the fabric of the communion, and is tearing The Episcopal

Church in America (TEC) and the Anglican Church of Canada (ACoC) apart. 200 bishops absented themselves from the Lambeth Conference 2008 because of the actions of these two denominations. The Presbyterian Church in the USA and the Lutheran Church are similarly divided, with new denominations arising. Does the Church of Ireland really want to risk dividing itself like this?

The original Anglican vision was for each national or particular church to be autonomous and culturally sensitive to 'divers habits', provided that everything was consonant with Scripture and served the purpose of edifying the church and promoting godliness (see the last paragraph of p17 BCP; and Article 34 on p786). What the reformers did not foresee was the English way of doing things being carried throughout the world by colonialism and missionary enterprise so that today the Anglican Communion has 38 autonomous Provinces, and over 80,000,000 members. Bishop Neill foresaw either a break-up of the Anglican Communion or a tightening of its central structures. Most of the old colonies had gained political independence and would soon assert their ecclesiastical independence. Would 'ties of affection' to Canterbury hold it together with the rise of divergent doctrines and practices? Not all Anglican Churches are equally loyal to our heritage, so he thought the Communion would be strained.

'Comprehensiveness' cannot extend forever without boundaries unless there are core doctrines and convictions. The Anglican Covenant is a valiant attempt to reinstate these convictions and repair the 'tear in the fabric' of the Communion, trying to balance autonomy and mutual interdependence of the member churches. Today's presenting issue concerns sexuality, but behind it are other issues of authority and accountability, interdependence and autonomy.

The current crisis in the Anglican Communion was triggered by the Consecration in 2003 of a partnered, openly homosexual man as Bishop of New Hampshire in the USA; and by the actions of the Canadian Diocese of New Westminster to authorize the blessings of same-sex unions. These actions were taken despite the pleas of the Global South Primates (Anglican Communion leaders; see the Kuala Lumpur Statement at www.globalsouthanglican.org and in the Appendices of this volume). The Communiqué of the Primates Meeting of 2002 stated that if ECUSA (now known as TEC) gave its consent and went ahead with the consecration, 'the fabric of the

Communion would be torn at the deepest level.' The Most Rev Frank Griswold (the Presiding Bishop of ECUSA at the time) nominally agreed with his fellow Primates, signed the document and then went home to consecrate the openly gay bishop anyway! In fact as Primate of ECUSA he was the chief consecrator.

Prior to these events, the Lambeth Conference of 1998 had been the biggest ever gathering of bishops in the Anglican Communion. Most were African. The previous Conference, at the suggestion of Rt. Rev. Dinis Singulane of Mozambique, had called for a Decade of Evangelism and that decade saw phenomenal growth in Africa. Uganda grew from 17 dioceses to 27. East African Bishops were routinely taking tea breaks in adult confirmation services because of the sheer numbers involved. The Church of Nigeria (which is part of the Anglican Communion) grew from 8 million members to 18 million. Today in Lagos, Nigeria, every Sunday there are more Anglicans in Church than in all of North America, the British Isles, Australia and New Zealand put together. By contrast, in America TEC membership has been steadily declining. On her election as Presiding Bishop Katherine Jefferts Schori attributed this to the education of Episcopalians and their concern not to over-populate the world, unlike irresponsible Roman Catholics and Mormons![3] With the mass exodus of conservative believers since 2003 TEC's membership has fallen below 2 million.

Many of the African Bishops were surprised and outraged that their colleagues in the West should put homosexuality on the agenda for the Lambeth Conference. It was only a small part of the whole conference, which was about the 'call to full humanity.' Resolution I.10 was passed by an overwhelming majority, affirming that marriage is the only place for sex and that all are created in God's image, loved by him and deserve dignity and respect. There was a commitment to sensitive listening to the experiences of homosexuals. It was further resolved that the Primates should continue the debate, having regard to the Kuala Lumpur Statement and other amendments that had been proposed by various African and Asian bishops. The Anglican Communion Office commented that a consensus had not yet been reached.

There are two different religions competing for the soul of our Communion. It is a struggle that has already been taking place for over 60 years in America (see Bishop Harold Miller's reflections on the American scene, Gazette August 2007).

One religion holds that Christ is the only Lord of his Church, and the Scriptures are God's Word, the sceptre of his rule, our only infallible rule and guide. This is not just the opinion of a particular party today but is classic Anglicanism as expressed in the 39 Articles, Hooker's Laws of Ecclesiastical Polity, John Jewel's Apologia pro Ecclesia Anglicana, Lambeth 1958 and the Windsor Report. The other religion holds that Jesus is merely an 'ikon of what we all aspire to be, a divine person.' 'To say he is unique is to put God in a small box.'[4] 'We decide what's in the Bible.'[5] 'The Bible is not God's Word but the record of the response of God's people to God's Word.'[6] One religion believes the Holy Spirit speaks through Scripture; the other believes "it" (must be gender neutral) works in every decision of Convention which in their subjective opinion is 'liberating and life-affirming.'[7]

Retired bishop Jack Spong of Newark in America claims Yahweh is a god cast in the image of a patriarchal society. He advocates not only the acceptance of same-sex unions but also temporary liaisons for pre-married and post-married people. Anyone who disagrees he dismisses as fearful and 'homophobic'. Paul, who was commissioned by the Risen Christ to bring about the obedience of faith from all nations is dismissed as a suppressed homosexual who couldn't relate to women.[8]

Both these competing religions see issues of sexuality as part of a wider debate. One sees behind it the doctrines of Biblical authority, creation, fall, sin, and repentance. The other sees it as part of a power struggle to maintain the position of male dominance and control. The choice before us is whether we uphold historic Anglicanism or not.

[1] Stephen Charles Neill, Anglicanism (Pelican Books, 1956) preface. The 1976 revised edition Oxford University Press does not have this preface, but does have an epilogue updating the Anglican situation (pp 399- 401), where he speaks of

theological and liturgical confusion because not all Anglican churches accept the two testaments, the three creeds, the four ecumenical councils, the 39 articles and the BCP as standards. Neill is describing what Anglicans accept rather than prescribing what they should accept.

[2] Canons of the Church of England

[3] New York Times magazine, November 19, 2006

[4] 'Ten questions for Katherine Jefferts Schori', Time magazine, July 2006. On TEC's website the Presiding Bishop has several sermons and articles. See www.trinitywallstreet.org

[5] John Shelby Spong, Living in Sin: a bishop rethinks sexual ethics (Doubleday, 1988) ch. 10

[6] Task Force on Sexuality, (Nevada General Convention 1988). Given as an appendix in Spong, ibid.

[7] Speeches at TEC General convention 2006

[8] Spong ibid. pp135ff. See also Spong chs. 8-10.

7

What will be our witness to Ireland?

A graduate in theology of Trinity College, Dublin, David Martin is currently an ordinand in part-time training with an interest in mission in Ireland.

Attitudes appear to be changing in the Church of Ireland, towards Lesbian, Gay, Bisexual and Transgender (LGBT) persons. But it is not only within churches that attitudes are changing of course. Within Irish culture, attitudes toward LGBT persons have changed too. From the decriminalisation of homosexuality in the in the early 1980s in Northern Ireland and a decade later in the Republic of Ireland, to the anti-discrimination legislation between 1998 and 2003, bringing us to the more recent Civil Union/Registered Partnership laws in the last six years, attitudes towards the LGBT community have come a long way.

The question is often asked as to whether or not the church should keep pace with such changes? But that, I think, can be really quite an unhelpful way of engaging with the issue. It seems to place the church on the back foot as it were, always having to react and respond. Instead, a more constructive way to proceed is to ask the question of the title to this article: as a church what will our witness be to Ireland? And in this brief attempt to answer the question I would like to address the three major stakeholders in the discussion: the homosexual community of Ireland; the heterosexual community of Ireland; and the future generations of Christians in Ireland.

Thus far, from the homosexual community's experience in Ireland, it appears that the church's witness has been, in the main, a hurtful one. Personal stories, that are increasingly well publicized are stacked up, rehearsing, what to the independent reader can only be perceived as a gross dereliction of duty on the church's behalf[1]. The church, most people intuitively sense, should be a place of welcome and acceptance, a place of love and forgiveness for all. It is shameful indeed when it appears that the culture is more Christian than the church. However, of course, any living church will have all these virtues and more. Yes, it will be welcoming and accepting of all. Love and forgiveness should be the hallmarks of its practice. But it will also be place of repentance and obedience for all who truly call on the name of the Lord. No one who claims to be following Christ has come to him free from sin. The reason anyone truly accepts his offer of forgiveness, to begin with, is because they see that they have been living for themselves and not for God. Moreover it appears central from what Jesus taught that he promises to change each and every one of us over the course of our lives. This is what every follower of Jesus signs up to. And throughout the teaching of the rest of the New Testament this is clearly applied no less to our sexual expression and attitudes as to our greed and gossip. To deny this would surely only eventually serve to silence the church's witness to the world. And this too, I would like to suggest, would be an equally gross dereliction of duty not only toward the homosexual community in Ireland, but indeed to all the communities in Ireland. If the church can only ever echo culture what will it have left to say for itself, or to culture? Sadly, today, to be part of a church that speaks and practices the truth in love means that the church increasingly is having to speak negatively against many moves that the culture seems intent on making. It makes our position increasingly difficult when the same negative comments must be made to those inside the church too. We owe the homosexual community nothing but the highest standards in purity and holiness, especially from our clergy.

Perhaps however it is because so many people from the homosexual community in Ireland have only ever experienced 'the truth' from heterosexual 'Christians', minus the love, that so many homosexuals have been hurt. Two things must be said in response. Firstly as Ed Vaughan points out in *What Some of You Were*, 'The Bible does not say, "Straight sex is good, gay sex is bad". Heterosexual adultery is no more or less of a sin than homosexuality. Christians do not argue for heterosexuality, but for obedience to God'. 'That,' he says, 'has implications for us all, no matter what our gender orientation.'[2] It certainly means issuing the call to repent to many more than just those who are listening as homosexuals in our communities and church. And this might even, secondly, begin to erode the accusation that as a church or even as certain groups within the church we are homophobic. We are not free to choose whom we are to love. And yes, as I have already said, that involves sticking wholeheartedly to the truth about sin and the need for forgiveness. However the context in which that issue is made surely must be one of deep compassion and care. The church's witness will come to nothing if it is not abundantly obvious that it is being done in love.

So, to conclude, as we think about our future, how will we be remembered by generations to come? What will be our witness as a church? Will we be remembered as those who jettisoned the truth in our day and denied our culture (and specifically the homosexual community) clear moral standards? As difficult and as offensive to some as it may be, will we deny this community what is ultimately for their best in the name of relevance and acceptance? Or perhaps we will be remembered as those who passed on by on the other side, worried that we might be perceived as being guilty by association. As demanding as it always is to genuinely care for others, will we jettison compassion and love in the name of truth? Surely would it not be better to be remembered as those who were both orthodox in their beliefs and lovingly radical in their practice? This I suggest is what our witness must be, for God's great glory and for the good of all.

---

[1] E.g. Revd Mervyn Kingston (ed.) *Share your story. Gay and Lesbian Experiences of Church.* (Changing Attitudes Ireland and the Church of Ireland Chaplaincy at TCD).
[2] Christopher Keane (ed.) *What some of you were. Stories about Christians and homosexuality*, (Liberty Christian Ministries, 2001). pp10-11

The
Biblical
Witness

8

"That's just your interpretation!"

Rev Eddie Coulter is the superintendent of Irish Church Missions and holds an MPhil in Biblical Studies from Queen's University, Belfast.

"That's just your interpretation! That's not how *I* read it. This is what *I* get out of the Bible passage." How many times have we heard this in a Bible study, discussion group or debate with someone about the meaning of a Bible passage? Or take another example: "You can make the Bible mean anything you want," the implication being that your opinion is not necessarily right just because you take that view. "There's lots of other interpretations, you know, and who's to say who's right?!" So, when it comes to debating what the Bible says on homosexuality (or indeed any subject), the conclusion is drawn that the very existence of a multiplicity of views is indication that there is no one right interpretation - just what's right for you and what's right for me.

If we start with the question, 'What does this Bible passage mean for me?', then naturally we will have as many interpretations as we have readers. But if we start with the question, 'What does this Bible passage mean?' before we look at its significance for us today, then we are more likely to find the right interpretation of it.[1] This is so because, as with any author of any book anywhere, the biblical authors are deliberately communicating a message to us. They have set out their material (revealed to them by the Holy Spirit) in their own style, but in such a way that they want us to see, hear, and understand clearly what God is saying. They don't want us to miss God's message. The right interpretation of a passage then, is finding out the author's intended meaning, not what we read into it.

So, how do we ensure that we get that message and don't end up interpreting the passage in a way it was never meant to be interpreted? Before we get to answering this, it is crucial to underline that we *can* understand Scripture and indeed that we are expected to understand (and obey) its plain message. The same Holy Spirit, who communicated God's message to the original writers of Scripture, is also at work to enlighten those who read. Therefore the Bible assures us that the right interpretation of Scripture is open to those whom the Spirit of God enlightens. This includes the person who is regenerate (1Corinthians 2:13-14); the person who is humble (Matthew 11:25-26); the person who is obedient (John 7:17; 14:21); and the person who listens to the Word in order to share Jesus with the world (Mark 4:21-25). In other words, a godly Christian, hungering and thirsting after righteousness and knowledge of God, seeking to make Christ known will be given understanding of the message. The Apostle Paul writes, 'Think over what I say for the Lord will give you understanding in everything' (2 Timothy 2:7)[2].

This is encouraging, but we are all aware that such biblical Christians do disagree over the text of Scripture on certain matters, for example infant baptism, church government, (ordained) women's ministry, or on understanding of the millennium (the reign of Christ for a thousand years). Surely, some may argue, if there can be genuine and acknowledged disagreement on the interpretation of Scripture on these matters (and Christians can peacefully live with this), why not on what the Bible says about homosexuality? Well, there is a difference. There are matters on which the Bible speaks more explicitly than others and upon which all biblical Christians agree[3]. This includes the central doctrines of faith and Christian morality. The Bible texts on homosexuality and the Gospel life all Christians are called to follow fall into this category. The sinfulness of a gay lifestyle (and love of God to save those sinners caught up in this lifestyle) is plainly taught in Scripture (1Corinthians 6:9-11): those raising their voice against this biblical view want to re-interpret Scripture by the presuppositions of a modern liberal society, thus reading into it what's not there.

This brings us then to the question of how we properly interpret Scripture, for the truth is, we are *all* tempted to read into Scripture what may not be there! All of us bring our presuppositions to the text and are in danger of making it say what is conducive to me in my culture and worldview[4]. How do we avoid this and get to the meaning of what the author is saying? Firstly, as we have discussed, the Bible is like no other book in that it is the divinely revealed Word of God and we study it like no other book in that we look to the Holy Spirit in prayer for understanding. However, since God has chosen to reveal His Word in human language, communicated at particular points in history in various forms of literary genre (e.g. narrative, prophecy, poetry, wisdom, apocalyptic), we must study it like any other book, paying close attention to its words and grammar, as well as the historical backgrounds of the original author and readers. This is a key part of the Holy Spirit's work in giving us understanding.

Therefore, to discover the meaning of any biblical text, we must examine the various contexts in which it is written. Firstly, we must examine the literary context. The meaning of words is found in the wider context of the sentences in which they are contained (not in the various meanings a dictionary tells us they can have). These sentences cannot be isolated from the paragraph in which they are situated and can only be properly comprehended when the flow of the paragraph is understood. Furthermore, such paragraphs are part of the author's overall argument in a book and thus the ideas flowing from its words and sentences conform to the purpose and main message of the book.

Part of that work of understanding the occasion (the reasons for the author writing) and the purpose of the book (the big message the author wants his readers to get), is to know something of the historical background. Just as the work of scholars in producing good translations help us understand the text, so too the work of scholars in producing Bible commentaries and dictionaries help us understand the historical background. But even this is not the whole story of understanding a text properly. The book or letter in which the passage is situated is part of a wider canonical or Biblical context. Each book of the Bible has something to contribute to the big message of the Bible, which is about God, redeeming and calling to Himself a people in Christ Jesus. Thus, through the diversity of biblical material there is an essential unity with the result that we cannot interpret one part of Scripture in such a way that it plainly contradicts another.[5]

The application of these principles of interpretation (exegesis), looking for the plain sense of Scripture to gather the author's intended meaning, will help us determine a more accurate hermeneutic, that is its meaning for us today. When applied to the Bible's teaching on homosexuality, Scripture cannot be interpreted to allow the gay lifestyle as a valid expression of Christian discipleship.

[1] For a useful discussion of this, see David Jackman, *Opening up the Bible.* (Bletchley, England: Scripture Union, 2006), pp.84-100
[2] John Stott, *Understanding the Bible,* (Reading: Scripture Union, 1984), pp.156-183
[3] Ibid, p.166 for a helpful understanding of how biblical Christians resolve matters where the meaning is not as apparently plain as others.
[4] Gordon D. Fee, Douglas Smith, *How to Read the Bible for All its Worth.* (Grand Rapids: Zondervan, 2003), pp. 17-31
[5] This is the teaching of Article 20 of the 39 Articles on what the church can and cannot change, and expresses the official position of the Church of Ireland on the unity of Scripture and its interpretation.

9

No longer relevant?
What does the Old Testament say?

Rev William Press is the Rector of Annalong, a member of General Synod and holds an MTh in Biblical Studies from Queen's University, Belfast.

The Old Testament clearly prohibits homosexual acts. However, revisionists within the Church are quick to point out that the OT also prohibits the wearing of polyester cotton shirts and the eating of shellfish. Christians do not follow these OT laws so why should we obey the ones regarding homosexuality? Should the Church, as is suggested, ignore these commands? Or are they still relevant?

In this short article I am going to argue that the Old Testament (as traditionally interpreted by Anglicans) is relevant to today's debate. Although NT teaching may be more immediate to our situation, living as we do on this side of the cross, the OT's commands are still able to inform us of the mind of God. The OT texts condemning homosexual acts are consistent with what we find in the NT and together they force us to conclude that the Scriptures as a whole firmly reject the practice.

'Not to abolish the Law'

In a crucial text for understanding the OT the Lord Jesus explains, 'I have not come to abolish the Law or the Prophets but to fulfil them' (Matthew 5:17). Clearly the coming of Jesus has changed the way Christians see the OT Law. In some sense he has fulfilled it – and we will see something of what this means below. At the same time, it has not been abolished. If it has not been abolished then it is still worth examining its instruction.

What does the OT say about homosexuality? The first main passage is found in Genesis 19:1-13 and is the notorious episode involving the ancient city of Sodom (a similar incident is found in Judges 19). The traditional Christian interpretation of this passage says that the men of Sodom were guilty of homosexual practices, which they attempted to inflict on two angels staying in Lot's home. Revisionists have challenged this interpretation by saying rather that the sin of Sodom was flouting the ancient rules of hospitality. The men of Sodom merely wanted to get acquainted with the visitors but should not have invaded Lot's home. Revisionists look to the OT prophets for support, who imply that Sodom's sin was hypocrisy, social injustice, deceit, arrogance and greed (e.g. Isaiah 1:10ff; Ezekiel 16:49ff).

However, the traditional reading needs little defending. Describing a breach of hospitality as 'wicked,' 'vile' and 'disgraceful' (Genesis 18:7; Judges 19:23) seems rather extreme (see also Ezekiel 16:50; 18:12; 33:26). Also, while the Hebrew verb 'to know' does not always refer to sexual intercourse, it does sometimes and is clearly used in this way in the Sodom story, where Lot's daughters are described as not having 'known' a man (Genesis 19:8). Homosexual behaviour may not have been Sodom's only sin, but according to Jude 7 it was certainly one of them.

Let's turn next to the two clearest OT commands concerning homosexual behaviour. They are both found in what is called the 'Holiness Code' in Leviticus. The first one, Leviticus 18:22, states simply, 'You shall not lie with a male as with a woman; it is an abomination.' Clearly, 'to lie with' includes the idea of sexual relations. The plain meaning of this command, however, is challenged by those who say it refers only to temple prostitutes and that its context is ritual uncleanness. It is not, they say, relevant to homosexual partnerships today.

Cult prostitution in the wider ancient Near Eastern context was the most (not the least) acceptable form of homosexual practice.[1] Certainly it is possible that some ancient Judeans participated in ritual homosexual practices associated with the cult of the goddess Asherah, even within the temple precincts. Probably some were homosexually oriented while others were not. Their practice was an 'abomination' (Deuteronomy 23:18; 1 Kings 14:24). However the Holiness Code should not only be taken to refer only to cult prostitutes. It was for all Israelites (not just priests) to keep their land unpolluted (not just the sanctuary).[2] The word 'abomination' is used elsewhere in the OT to include idolatry (Deuteronomy 7:25-26), sorcery (Deuteronomy 18:9-12), adultery (Ezekiel 18:6), incest (Ezekiel 22:10-11) and cross-dressing (Deuteronomy 22:5), to name but a few. It is not restricted to temple prostitution and always expresses God's displeasure.

'But to fulfil it'

We will consider the second Leviticus reference now, remembering Jesus' claim to fulfil the Law. Leviticus 20:13 states not just the prohibition of homosexual acts but also the punishment: 'If a man lies with a male as with a woman, both of them have committed an abomination; they shall surely be put to death; their blood is upon them.' Having read this, we might be having some sympathy with the revisionist position! However, the coming of Jesus has changed how God's people should read a verse like this.

Every text has its context. The context for these verses in Leviticus is the children of Israel in the wilderness. Israel is about to enter the promised land of Canaan. Leviticus 18 explains that God is going to drive the Canaanites out of the land because they have been committing the same sort of sexual immorality which the chapter now condemns (vv1-3). God was clearly indicating that his ancient people were to have different standards of behaviour than their surrounding culture.

So is this text of any relevance today? The punishment in ancient Israel was death but since Jesus has come this punishment has been revoked.[3] 'Let him who is without sin cast the first stone!' instructed Jesus about the woman caught in adultery (John 8:7). Since none of us is without sin it is not up to Christians today to punish anyone in that way. It will be up to God alone to implement any judgment on the last day. As Christians we are to be compassionate to everyone struggling with sexual temptation while not condoning the sin. 'Go and sin no more', was how Jesus concluded his encounter with the woman. The homosexual practice described in Leviticus 18:22 and 20:13 is still to be condemned while the punishment is not to be enforced.

A common argument put forward today for ignoring these laws in Leviticus is as follows. 'Of course there are laws against homosexuality in the Old Testament. But there are also curious laws about abstaining from pork and not wearing clothing made from two types of material. Christians don't keep those laws so why keep the homosexuality one?'

The answer is that there are different types of law in the Old Testament. In fact all the laws can be classified in three categories: there are ceremonial laws (e.g. to do with making ritual, animal sacrifices); there are cultural laws that mark out God's people from the other nations (e.g. not eating pork); and there are moral laws (e.g. 'love your neighbour').

Traditionally, Anglicans have recognised these categories: ceremonial, cultural and moral. We have regarded the first two as being fulfilled by Christ, while the third has on-going relevance for the behaviour of God's (NT-) people.[4]

Article VII of the Thirty-Nine Articles (found in the Church of Ireland's Book of Common Prayer) says: 'Although the Law given from God by Moses, as touching Ceremonies and Rites, do not bind Christian men, nor the Civil precepts thereof ought of necessity to be received in any commonwealth; yet notwithstanding, no Christian man whatsoever is free from the obedience of the Commandments which are called Moral.'

How do we know that the OT laws condemning homosexual acts should be classified as moral? Because the NT never treats sexual practices as ceremonial or cultural. In fact the condemnation of homosexual practice continues without exception into the NT. These OT laws are not ceremonial or cultural, which would mean they would cease to apply (e.g. Mark 7:19; Acts 10:9-16). They are clearly moral and hence have continuing relevance.

Conclusion
Surely the Church of Ireland does not wish to reject God's OT laws or the traditional way it has interpreted them. They are a revelation of the mind of God and the moral laws are as relevant today as they ever have been. If we disregard the OT moral laws on homosexuality what does this say about our love for Scripture as a whole?

[1] Robert Gagnon, *The Bible and Homosexual Practice*, (Nashville: Abingdon Press, 2001) p44-54

[2] Ibid. p111

[3] See David Huss' comments in the next chapter.

[4] In a sense Christ has fulfilled the moral law also, inasmuch as he kept it perfectly.

10
Did Jesus have a view on same-sex unions?

A graduate of the university of Oxford, the Rev David Huss is Rector of the Donegal group of parishes.

A few years ago, there was a trend among some Christians to wear bracelets emblazoned with the letters 'WWJD'. It stood for 'What would Jesus do?' – a great question to ask when we are faced with a difficult choice or tricky moral question.

What would Jesus do, or say, about same-sex unions? Two statements are commonly made: first, that Jesus, in the Gospels, was silent on the issue of homosexuality; and second, that if he had addressed the topic, he would have affirmed committed, permanent, same-sex unions, since he always showed love and acceptance, even towards those treated as outcasts by conventional religious opinion.

If these two claims are true, they would form a powerful case for the acceptance of sexually active same-sex partnerships within the Church of Ireland today. But are they true? We need to examine each statement carefully.

Claim 1: Jesus was silent on the subject of homosexuality
At first sight, the statement seems quite correct. Nowhere in the four Gospels do we find any record of Jesus specifically discussing homosexuality or dealing with homosexual people. Do we then have no trace of his viewpoint on the subject?

We need to look a little harder. Jesus lived and spoke within a first-century Jewish culture in which any form of sexual intercourse between two people of the same sex was regarded as sinful (in line with the consistent view of the Old Testament writers). Of course, Jesus did not always go along with the views of his fellow first-century Jews. For example, on the subject of the Sabbath law and the laws regarding 'kosher' food, he was not afraid to take a more liberal stance than the religious leaders of his day. But in these cases he gave clear teaching to indicate that he took a different view. If Jesus differed from the consensus of his time regarding homosexual practice, he left no evidence at all to indicate it. In the absence of such evidence, it makes sense to assume that Jesus agreed with the prevailing opinion of his time.

Indeed, when we look at what Jesus did teach on the subject of sexual morality, we find that, rather than being more liberal than the religious opinion-setters of his time, he was in fact stricter. This is seen most clearly in the passages in which Jesus debates with the Pharisees on the subject of divorce. We read in Mark 10:

> *Some Pharisees came, and to test him they asked, 'Is it lawful for a man to divorce his wife?' He answered them, 'What did Moses command you?' They said, 'Moses allowed a man to write a certificate of dismissal and to divorce her.' But Jesus said to them, 'Because of your hardness of heart he wrote this commandment for you. But from the beginning of creation, "God made them male and female." "For this reason a man shall leave his father and mother and be joined to his wife, and the two shall become one flesh." So they are no longer two, but one flesh. Therefore what God has joined together, let no one separate.' Then in the house the disciples asked him again about this matter. He said to them, 'Whoever divorces his wife and marries another commits adultery against her; and if she divorces her husband and marries another, she commits adultery.'*
> Mark 10:2-12 (NRSV).

My purpose here is not to deal with the complex subject of divorce and remarriage, but to point out firstly that Jesus was considerably stricter in his approach to sexual morality than most, if not all, of the religious teachers of his age.

Secondly, these verses show that, when dealing with the subject of marriage, Jesus took as his starting point 'the beginning of creation,' in other words the situation spelled out in the opening chapters of the book of Genesis.

Jesus twice quotes from these chapters in his discussion of the true nature of marriage. From Genesis 1:27 he highlights the distinct creation of human beings as male and female. From Genesis 2:24 he gleans the authoritative description of marriage: a man leaves his own family, is united to his wife and the two are joined together by God as 'one flesh'.

Jesus' teaching on marriage is summed up very well in the official documents of the Church of Ireland:

> *The Church of Ireland affirms, according to our Lord's teaching, that marriage is in its purpose a union permanent and life-long, for better or worse, till death do them part, of one man with one woman, to the exclusion of all others on either side...*
> From Canon 31.1 from Chapter IX of the Constitution of the Church of Ireland

We see now that although Jesus did not specifically address the subject of homosexuality, that does not mean he said nothing relevant to the topic. On the contrary, he addressed head-on the central issue at stake: the question of how human beings are to use their sexuality in line with God's loving purposes in creation. Jesus taught that the proper context for sex is lifelong, heterosexual marriage.

Claim 2: Jesus would have affirmed loving, committed same-sex unions

Again, at first sight this statement seems compelling. No-one could possibly read the four Gospels and deny that Jesus was the most wonderfully loving and welcoming person who has ever lived. He shared meals with tax-collectors and prostitutes, even when this caused a scandal to the conservative religious leadership of the time. Surely he would show the same welcome and acceptance towards practising homosexuals today, particularly those in committed, long-term relationships?

We must, however, remember what we have already seen – that in his teaching Jesus never overturned any Old Testament law regarding sexual morality. Although he did set aside or soften the laws on the Sabbath and on food, he took a stronger, rather than a weaker, line on sexual matters.

Only in one respect did Jesus soften the Old Testament approach to sexual sin – he overturned the use of the death penalty as a punishment. In the famous story from John 8 of the woman caught in adultery, Jesus effectively prevented the crowds from stoning her (as the OT law in fact required) and instead set her free. This is a powerful reminder that violence against homosexual people (or any other group) is utterly abhorrent and must be strenuously avoided by Christians.

After saving the woman's life, Jesus gave her an opportunity for a second chance, telling her, 'Go on your way, and from now on do not sin again' (John 8:11b NRSV). This command to 'sin no more' indicates the probable attitude of Jesus towards all who were engaged in sexual immorality. Much as he associated with them, ate with them and saved them from execution, he also expected them to change their behaviour. Jesus may have eaten with prostitutes, but he also expected them to give up prostitution.

One clue to the likely attitude of Jesus towards sexually immoral behaviour comes from his approach to tax-collectors. When, in Luke 19, Jesus invited himself to the home of Zacchaeus, the chief tax-collector notorious for defrauding the people, he rejoiced when Zacchaeus offered to pay back fourfold whatever he had wrongly taken, giving clear evidence of his repentance. His experience of the welcome of Jesus led to a radical change of behaviour.

Still today, Jesus offers welcome and forgiveness for all sinners. No-one is beyond the scope of his saving love. But there is a cost to following Christ; our lives must be surrendered to him and our obedience must be unconditional. None of us can expect our behaviour to go unchallenged by his searching demands.

Conclusion
So, the two claims often made in regard to Jesus' attitude to homosexuality are found to be lacking: in regard to the first claim, we have seen that Jesus did in fact say things which are relevant to the subject, particularly when he endorsed Genesis' view of marriage as a permanent, monogamous and heterosexual union. At the same time, he said nothing to indicate a softening of the Old Testament's prohibition of same-sex intercourse.

All of this makes it highly unlikely that the second claim (that Jesus would affirm same-sex partnerships) is true. Although Jesus would undoubtedly have sought to befriend and be hospitable towards homosexual people, there is no reason to think he would have endorsed the active, physical expression of homosexual desire. More likely, he would have expected repentance from those engaged in such actions.

We began with the question – what would Jesus do? The answer is now clear: he would have shown kindness and love towards homosexual people. He would have listened to them and eaten with them. And he would have lovingly but clearly called on them to abstain from the sin of homosexual intercourse and instead, by his help, to live a life of purity. Our calling is to do the same.

11

In context. What does the (rest of the) New Testament say?

A former university chaplain, the Rev Trevor Johnston is Crosslinks Ireland Team Leader and a member of General Synod.

Does the New Testament address homosexuality? On face value, the answer is yes. Is it addressed positively or negatively? On face value, the answer is negatively. But therein lies the problem. For some, 'on face value' doesn't convince. After all, is the homosexual behaviour of the Apostle Paul's day understood in the same way as it is today? Wasn't it uncommitted or abusive relationships that Paul criticised? Isn't it superficial to conclude that the NT's writers dismissed loving and committed same-sex relationships? Weren't they homophobic and ignorant of both science and psychology? Words have different meanings in different places and times, therefore, knowing precisely what they meant more than twenty centuries later is difficult, if not impossible. These questions are serious. They challenge the traditional understanding of human sexuality. Indeed, these questions, and similar, challenge other things taken to be central to the Christian faith.

The purpose of this essay is to examine some of the significant New Testament texts within which homosexuality is considered. At the outset it is important to acknowledge that each party in the current debate has their own agenda when approaching these texts. Surely the most honest approach is to humbly bow before the texts and let them speak on their own terms? In order to do full justice to them and recognise possible bias, the immediate and wider contexts surrounding the texts will be taken into consideration.

Outside the four Gospels, there are several passages in the New Testament in which homosexuality is referred. There are three main categories:

1) Reference to homosexuality is implied[1];
2) Homosexuality is listed amongst other sins such as slander and non-married sexual activity in so-called 'vice lists'[2];
3) Reference to homosexuality/lesbianism forms a substantial element of an argument[3].

1)   The first category is effectively represented by a passage such as Jude 7 (with echoes in 2 Peter 2:4-7 & 10). It makes reference to the sexual 'immorality' of Sodom and Gomorrah. The incident referred to is the men of Sodom seeking sexual relations with male visitors to their city[4]. These visitors were angels sent by God, who were embodied as men, to investigate whether the outcry against the cities' sin was accurate. Some suggest that Sodom's main sin was inhospitality[5] – that the visitors were not treated as they ought to have been, thus provoking God's anger (and fire) because etiquette and good manners were not observed. This view provides an understanding of God that is hard to reconcile with the rest of the Scriptures. Others suggest that it was the flesh of *angels* not humans which interested the men of Sodom[6]. Thus, their sin was in seeking sexual intercourse with non-humans. However, the population of the twin cities did not know they were angels. The texts of Genesis 19 and its interpretation later in the Bible and within other, later non-Biblical material make this clear[7]. Still others suggest that it was homosexual *rape*, not, primarily, a loving stable relationship which received God's disapproval. However, this text is placed within Genesis, which espouses a male-female basis for intercourse from the creation story onwards. It is hard to imagine that the male-male nature of this sexual encounter would have received approval.

2)   In the second category, Paul is the main writer of the texts under consideration. Of course, views of the Apostle are influenced by our 21st century context – perhaps, the first context that we must acknowledge is our own. He is typically portrayed as: a hater of women; a promoter of slavery; a first century homophobe and the founder of a legalistic religion of law keeping, contrary to the religion of love and freedom that Jesus established. Of course, simple

examination of his texts will see that, in actual fact, Paul has not invented another religion. He suggests that women ought to be the objects of their husbands' self-sacrificing devotion and that love is the hallmark of godly human relationships. Slaves of his day are to honour their masters and masters are to be merciful to their slaves.

Thus, our attention turns to the vice lists. Some involved in the debate make much of the fact that the words associated with homosexual behaviour appear merely in lists. Ironically, they suggest, this simple or cursory reporting implies that Paul is intentionally making little of each of the behaviours itemised. This is a false trail. Surely, complete omission would successfully make little of it? Inclusion on a list increases, not diminishes, its significance. No one would suggest that love is diminished because it appears within a list of (for example) the fruit of the Spirit. A full treatment on a singular behaviour is not necessary or fitting with the author's intention.

The wider context for one list, which appears in 1 Corinthians 6:9-11, is Paul's rebuke to the Corinthian Christians for the misuse of the body. The Corinthian's culturally influenced understanding of the body devalued it and caused it to have secondary importance to the soul. They also had confusion around the issue of the boundaries of Christian freedom. The specific issue is an incestuous relationship that doesn't appear to bother the Corinthians, since they make no judgment about it or effort to discipline those involved. Thus, Paul reminds the Corinthians that there *are* those who will be excluded from the Kingdom of God, but that the behaviours listed have now been forgiven and the participants made clean – the Corinthians 'were' some of those who previously had participated in them. Modern Bible translations have differing approaches to these two Greek words included in this 'vice list' which reference same-sex sexual activity. This does not mean that the meaning is obscure or essentially in dispute; rather, approaches to the best way to *phrase* the meaning of these two words, in English, is varied.

The two words essentially describe the two aspects of a same-gender, consensual, sexual relationship. The first word[8] means 'soft men' or 'men who feminise themselves to attract male sex partners' (the female role). This is then paired with a word[9] that appears to be constructed by Paul in which he draws together two Greek words – 'male' (*arsen*) and 'lying' (*koite*). Therefore, it literally means, 'men lying with a male' (the male role). The context doesn't suggest male prostitution or exploitation. The fact that these two words appear together suggests neither coercion nor uncommitted sexual encounters. They are simply the two sexual parts within homosexual activity, where two males enact the female and male roles.

3)   The third category, where significant reference to same-gender sexual activity forms a major element of the argument, is represented within the opening chapter of Paul's letter to the Romans[10]. Some claim that these verses refer to sexual exploitation in the form of rape, prostitution or pederasty (sexual activity between a man and a boy). It is claimed that Paul was not aware of either sexual orientation (homosexual or heterosexual) or loving and committed same-gender relationships.   However, these arguments must be challenged.

The wider context in the opening verses of Romans is the human propensity to suppress the truth about God and choose to worship not the Creator, but creation – to believe lies rather than admit the obvious truth of a Creator. He is echoing the pattern established in the Garden of Eden, namely, the serpent deceives Eve and Adam disobeys God having been led by his wife – creature obeying creation, rather than Creator.   Humanity, Paul claims, prefers to deny the existence of God, despite seeing the evidence of the created order. The wrath of God has been provoked (1:18). As a result, humanity has been handed over to its rebellious desires. Included in this is the 'handing over' of males and females to same-gender sexual activity. Humanity suppresses the *obvious* truth about God in such a way that even the use of the body in homosexual relationships denies its unmissable and fully discernible anatomical structure.

Some argue that when Paul uses 'natural' in these verses, he is ignorant of sexual orientation; thus saying that homosexuality is unnatural for those who are, by *orientation*, heterosexual. This is misleading; as the thrust of his main argument is that the Creator has ordered creation in a certain way and humanity has suppressed this ordering. Therefore, those who claim, 'God made me this way', fail to acknowledge how the male and female bodies are physically structured, in both physiological and psychological compatibility. Moreover, the words that he uses are within the category of desire – it is hard to detach this from 'orientation'. After all, even heterosexuals can desire those with whom they are not in a married bond: enacting and continuing that lust is certainly forbidden for the Christian.

Furthermore, it is difficult to sustain that Paul had exploitative or coercive relationships in mind, since women also exchanged natural relations with men for those with women. Long-term, committed homosexual relationships were a feature of early Greek and Roman culture, including semi-official 'marriages' between men and between women. It is untrue to say that Paul was either unaware or tacitly approving of same-gender relationships. In an article, Professor Robert Gagnon cites Louis Crompton, a homosexual scholar, when acknowledging this very point[11]:

> 'However well-intentioned the interpretation that Paul's words were not directed at 'bona fide' homosexuals in committed relationships… [this] seems strained and unhistorical. Nowhere does Paul or any other Jewish writer of this period imply the least acceptance of same-sex relations under any circumstance. The idea that homosexuals might be redeemed by mutual devotion would have been wholly foreign to Paul or any other Jew or early Christian.'[12]

Commitment does not change the unnatural character of a relationship. The exchange is equal between men and women. Paul roots his argument in the creation accounts of Genesis 1 and 2. He is not reflecting a culturally or personally biased position against homosexuals. Instead, he roots his understanding in the genesis of everything at creation, as the true and living God has determined it.

It is hard not to notice a monumental shift in the secular world's attitude towards homosexuality over the past few decades. In particular, over the past fifteen years there has been a major public campaign to gain acceptance for homosexuality – this has now been mooted in the UK. Legalizing same-sex marriage has become the end goal of the campaign to equate homosexuality with heterosexuality. It is hard not to acknowledge that for the Church to remain faithful to her apostolic roots, resisting this revisionism is the only option. The New Testament does address the issue of homosexuality and is internally consistent on this issue. It acknowledges its Old Testament roots, strengthens them and maintains clear continuity with the principles found therein. This brief survey highlights this convergence. Traditional Christian belief has been soundly argued throughout the centuries. May the church of Jesus Christ continue to hear her Lord's voice as it has been revealed in his Word.

[1] Especially Jude 7. See also 2 Peter 2:6-7, 10, Revelation 21:27 and Revelation 22:15

[2] 1 Corinthians 6:9-11 and 1 Timothy 1:9-10

[3] Romans 1:24-27

[4] Genesis 19:4-11

[5] D. Sherwin Bailey has predominantly advanced this view. Yet as Derek Kidner points out, in his commentary on Genesis, the conclusion forwarded by 'Dr Bailey has traveled more widely than the reasons he produces for it.' Derek Kidner, *Tyndale Old Testament Commentaries: Genesis* (Leicester: IVP, 1963) p137

[6] e.g. L William Countryman & MR Riley, *Gifted by otherness: gay and lesbian Christians in the Church* (Harrisburg: Morehouse Publishing, 2001) p35

[7] The literature associated with 2nd Temple Judaism condemns homosexual practice.

[8] *malakoi (English transliteration)*

[9] *arsenokoitai (English transliteration)*

[10] Romans 1:24-27

[11] Robert Gagnon, "Going in the wrong direction: a response to David Atkinson", found at http://www.fulcrum-anglican.org.uk/page.cfm?ID=314

[12] L Crompton, *Homosexuality and Civilisation* (Harvard: Harvard University Press, 2003) p114

Pastoral Relationships

12

Pastoral care of gay people and their families

Rev Canon David McClay is the Rector of Willowfield Parish, Belfast, a member of General Synod and the leader of the New Wine network in Ireland.

Caring for people at all stages of life and with all kinds of need has always been one of the pillars of the Christian church, back to the very earliest days of Acts. Even then it was not always straightforward, with the apostles needing to bring in deacons to help with what we might now call 'Pastoral ministry.' We see a model of care that was inclusive, practical, down-to-earth and focused on those on the edge of the church.

I want to encourage us to think about the great opportunity that the tradition of pastoral care offers us to reach out to those who are on the edge of church life today, with genuine care and acceptance. If we do that we will find that we have the opportunity to pastor people who are struggling in many areas of life – finance, alcohol and other addictions, loneliness, grief, unemployment and also sexuality. We have a gospel that brings wholeness and forgiveness, transformation and the power to live lives that are holy. Each individual struggling with any issue needs and deserves our best care and prayers, but also deserves us to speak truth and grace into their life as they try to resolve the issue they face.

It is one of the wonderful privileges of Christian ministry both ordained and lay to come alongside people as they find God in the midst of life's disappointments, hurts, grief, confusion and struggles with temptation. Life is complex and when we think and talk about pastoral care in today's world our thinking cannot be limited to visiting the sick, the elderly and the bereaved, important as these are.

Where the church is already engaging with peoples' needs in a local parish and community context there will be a wide range of pastoral issues that arise. People will be real about the life issues that they face when they realise that they are accepted and cared about. We must begin by being intentional about creating a culture of welcome where people find it natural to be open, real and honest about their hopes, dreams, fears, struggles and temptations.

John tells us that 'the word became flesh and made his dwelling among us. We have seen his glory, the glory of the One and Only, who came from the Father, full of grace and truth' (John 1:14). Today's church needs to be intentional about being incarnational, among people, with people, enabling people to see who God is, what God is like and the life to which He calls us. We need to be among people enabling them to own and experience God's grace and God's truth. God's grace and God's truth do not contradict each other. In every pastoral situation we need to be carriers of both God's truth and His grace.

In a church culture where grace and truth are present men and women will discover they can be real about how they are struggling with their sexual identity or with same-sex attraction. They will find freedom to express their confusion as to whether they are gay or straight. It is actually a very small percentage of the population who conclude they are gay but many more at some stage do struggle with issues around sexual identity. When people know those coming alongside them are people who genuinely care about them and won't judge them, they will be comfortable to talk through any struggles including sexual struggles. Exposure to God's word as we guide people to the scriptures, along with prayer ministry, will often lead to that person choosing to begin living for Christ.

At Willowfield we have found that a course called 'Romance Academy' available from *Love for Life* gives young people aged 14+ a solid biblical and wholesome foundation to help them deal with issues such as relationships, love, sex, sexual health, sexual relationships and other related issues.

We need to acknowledge that much work remains to be done in all our churches by way of creating a culture of welcome where all feel welcome but where the grace and truth that characterised Jesus is found in the culture and life of our local parish churches.

In a church where there is a culture of welcome and where grace and truth abound we will find ourselves having honest conversations with those who may describe themselves as gay or lesbian. In my experience of pastoral ministry people have real questions that it is our responsibility to attempt to answer honestly. And it is so much better if those questions can be asked in an environment that offers biblical truth, grace-filled boundaries and a gospel that doesn't bring condemnation but forgiveness, freedom and transformation.

Where there is a church culture that is welcoming and inclusive and a biblical framework that faces difficult issues with both truth and grace, the grace and truth that came through Jesus Christ those who are gay or who struggle with same sex attractions will ask tough questions. In my experience the questions we will be asked will include: "Can someone help me say No to my desire as a man to have sex with other men?"

The answer to this person will include someone coming alongside him who will listen to his struggles, enable him to know God's love and purposes for his life. This person needs to be someone who will regularly pray with him and ask tough questions to help him avoid falling into temptation. It is important that he understands that temptation in itself is not sinful. It only becomes sin when we give in to the temptation.

Another question we are asked goes something like this: "I've slept with someone of the same sex and I feel so guilty. Will God forgive me? Am I gay?" This person too will need ongoing support and assurance that Jesus' death on the cross enables us to find cleansing from any sin. Sex with someone of the same gender is no more and no less sinful than sex outside of marriage between a heterosexual couple. God is always willing to forgive us for all our sins. As in many situations, ongoing accountability will enable this person to move forward and live a life that honours God.

When someone comes to the church saying: "I've had several gay partners over many years but I want to change my lifestyle and I want to give my life to Christ," it is our privilege as always to lead that person to trust personally in Christ, for a whole new beginning. But with that privilege comes the ongoing responsibility to provide them with the level of support, friendship and accountable, pastoral care needed to help them grow in their walk with God.

When people choose to live a celibate life in order to avoid sexual sin or for other reasons the church needs to ensure that all who are single are valued and included in the church's ministries and church family.

I have heard some who would describe themselves as gay, but who with God's strength and the support of a church family and close Christian friends are choosing to live a celibate life make comments like: "I will feel so let down if the church says that practising a gay sexual lifestyle is acceptable." These courageous men and women need reassurance that the Church's biblical and historic teaching on sexuality and marriage will remain unaltered. They often find it painful and difficult to deal with the intolerance of some who push a very liberal agenda.

In the church we need to see it as part of our pastoral ministry to ensure we are helping men and women deal with same sex attractions by supporting them in saying no to sexual intimacy with people of the same gender. Indeed we ought to strengthen all our people to say no to sexual intimacy outside of marriage.

Equally, in pastoral ministry some of us have been there to help people live with HIV Aids and tragically to help others dying of AIDS – contracted when they were in a gay or heterosexual relationship. Again we need to ensure that people who face such painful and tragic circumstances have much by way of loving support and that we help them face death knowing the assurance of a grace and truth-filled 'Holy Catholic Church,' as well as 'the communion of saints, the resurrection of the body and the life everlasting.' We are always a people of hope. As the late David Watson said shortly before his death, "The best is yet to be!" In many parishes the church needs to relearn how to lead all our people into repentance, into confessing faith in Christ and into the assurance of God's pardon and peace and into the life that is life in all its fullness.

As well as helping those who are gay live for Christ the church needs to be much more engaging in how we pastor and mentor all of our people in pursuing lives where our sexual behaviour both honours Christ and is God's best for each individual. I have yet to meet a couple who chose to avoid sexual intercourse prior to marriage who regretted that decision, but I have seen and helped people deal with the pain that results in sex outside of a faithful marriage between one man and one woman.

It will be a church culture as well as a theology that is characterised by truth and grace that will help us pastor all our people single and married, gay or straight, divorced or widowed to find Christ and live lives that will glorify God and enjoy him forever.

13

Follow the Leader!
Setting a godly example to teens

Johnny Beare has had many years experience in Christian youth work and is currently the youth worker at St Elizabeth's Parish Church, Belfast.

Youth leaders are renowned for their icebreaker games, which are played at the start of many youth groups. One such icebreaker game is 'Follow the Leader,' a fun copy-cat game in which people try and imitate a leader's actions.

If truth be told, all youth ministry could be classed as a continuous game of 'Follow the Leader'. As church leaders seek to prayerfully teach the Word of God to teenagers, it is important that they also model what they teach in their lives. When Paul was instructing Timothy on how he should lead God's people he said: 'Be an example to all believers in what you say, in the way you live, in your love, your faith, and your purity.' (1 Timothy 4:12b NLT). It is vitally important that church leaders set believers (including teenagers) a godly example in what they say, in the way they live, in their love, their faith and their purity (including sexual purity). To teach well involves much more than merely using words. It involves leaders 'modelling' their teaching to young people and asking young people to 'Follow the Leader.'

Ephesians is a great Bible book for teaching to teenagers. It is short, snappy and contains a perfect balance between doctrine and practical teaching. Chapters 1-3 will open a young person's eyes to the great plan of God and help them see how they fit into it. He or she will also hear the most astonishing truth which says, 'Once you were dead because of your disobedience and many sins...But God is so rich in mercy, and he loved us so much, that even though we were dead because of our sins, he gave us life when he raised Christ from the dead. It is only by God's grace you have been saved!' (Ephesians 2:1, 4-5 NLT). This is the gospel message we want to communicate carefully, attractively, clearly and at a level young people can grasp and respond to.

But, how should young people respond to this glorious news of God's love, mercy and grace? Paul tells his readers their response should be to 'throw off your old sinful nature and your former way of life, which is corrupted by lust and deception.' (Ephesians 4:22 NLT). Instead, these young Christians in Ephesus are told, 'Imitate God in everything you do, because you are his dear children. Live life filled with love following the example of Christ. He loved us and offered himself as a sacrifice for us and offered himself as a sacrifice for us, a pleasing aroma to God. Let there be NO sexual immorality, impurity, or greed among you. Such sins have NO place among God's people' (Ephesians 5:1-3 NLT).

A young person responding to the good news of the gospel must be challenged to throw off the sin that has characterised their old way of life and lead a new life which reflects God's nature and God's word. Paul is clear that in this new life there should be no hint of sexual sin (sexual behaviour outside of marriage between one man and one woman), no hint of impurity and no hint of greed. This is a tough call for young people, when one considers, 'It is estimated that the average person is exposed to about 14,000 sexual messages per year (just under 40 per day), and less than 200 of those 14,000 advise caution or hesitation about sex.'[1] Therefore, this one area where young people need to see a godly example and where they need to be able to 'Follow the Leader'.

It is the job of Christian parents, youth leaders, church leaders, bishops, select vestry members, synods people and all Christians to ensure young people are receiving the teaching they need to hear and the godly example they need to follow, in the area of sex and relationships.

Bible Teaching
The world's view of relationships between men and women is very different from God's original plan for us. It can be very easy for young people (and adults) to become so rooted in the culture of the

day that they no longer see the problems with it. The world is setting young people an example that says, 'If it feels right just do it.' But this example is causing many young people to pursue a lifestyle leading them away from God and his plan for them. That is why what the Bible says about sex and relationships is one of those topics that church leaders should be revisiting frequently with their young people.[2] It is vitally important churches ensure that young people are taught God's plan for sex as revealed in His Word, making every effort to clear up any confusion which may lead young people towards eternity-jeopardising behaviour, and demonstrating that willful rebellion against God's word has no place amongst God's people. This is one of the reasons that the church must be very clear about its teaching on marriage; there is no room for ambiguity because the consequences of any misunderstanding are far too serious.

Godly Example

As stated above, to teach the Bible well involves more than words. It involves 'modelling' Bible-centred behaviour for young people to follow. Nowhere is this more important than in the whole area of relationships. Young people need to be around people championing and modelling God's plan for marriage: 'Wives submitting to husbands as to the Lord,…and husbands loving wives as Christ loved the church' (Ephesians 5:22, 25 NLT). For young people there is nothing more damaging than church leaders teaching one thing with their words and another thing with their actions; or church leaders being one thing in public and something very different in private. Charles Swindoll in his book on Grace puts it this way:

> 'You want to mess up the minds of your children? Here's how - guaranteed! Rear them in a legalistic, tight context of external religion, where performance is more important than reality. Fake your faith. Sneak around and pretend your spirituality. Train your children to do the same. Embrace a long list of do's and don'ts publicly but hypocritically practice them privately . . . yet never own up to the fact that its hypocrisy. Act one way but live another. And you can count on it - emotional and spiritual damage will occur.'[3]

It is of the utmost importance that church leaders model the Bible's teaching on sex and relationships in a way that is authentic and transparent. That is part of the reason it is totally incompatible for a church leader to be, on the one hand a minister in a church that holds to the Bible's teaching on marriage, and on the other hand part of a civil partnership. Such an example just leads to utter confusion in the minds of the young people to whom God calls us to proclaim the gospel.

Intentionally or otherwise, young people will always play 'Follow the Leader', and therefore church leaders must be very careful to guard both their life and doctrine, so as not to lead young people astray. It is the duty of every Christian to ensure they are both teaching in word and example what God has said, and calling themselves and others to repent when word and action no longer underpin each other.

---

[1] Scott Perry *Little Black Book: Sex.* (The Good Book Company, 2009) p7
[2] A great resource for teaching young people is 'Sex and Relationships' by Roger Fawcett (TnT Ministries). It contains 6 youth group sessions on sex and relationships, and is available from www.thegoodbook.co.uk
[3] Charles Swindoll. *The Grace Awakening.* (Dallas: Word Pub. 1990) p97

14
Listening to all sides – the witness of a celibate, homosexual Christian

As we have seen, the debate to which this book seeks to contribute is benefited enormously by considered reflection on the Biblical texts. It is clear that homosexual relationships, even 'monogamous' ones, are contrary to God's design for marriage and to reject such teaching is to reject God's authority and revealed will for human sexual intimacy.

However, the debate is weakened if we do not regard the testimony of those who accept the Bible's teaching on human sexuality, yet experience homosexual desires and choose to live celibate lives. I am one such person.

For over a decade now my faith and my homosexual desire have walked hand in hand, they were both awakened at the age of thirteen and have wrestled with one another ever since. I was converted out of a non-Christian family because of the witness of Christian friends and the testimony of an 'elderly' (at least, I thought he was elderly) Christian man who taught the midweek Bible class a friend had dragged me along to.

I began to see Jesus for who he really was, that he died to bring rebels into the family of God, to turn enemies into sons and to love them as a gracious father. In short, Jesus changed my heart.

Around the same time I began to notice that there was something different about me. My friends had begun to notice girls, there was the typical teenage chatter about who liked who, coupled with the politics of trying to negotiate a fleeting (yet all-consuming) relationship with a member of the opposite sex. During such conversations I tended to keep a low profile, trying to avoid giving an answer. I had no idea which girl was more attractive nor did I care; and as time went on I began to realise there was something terribly wrong.

My inability to speak to my Christian friends or leaders about my homosexuality led very quickly to feelings of difference and loneliness. I began to 'medicate' myself with pornography, fantasy and masturbation. This continued from fourteen to nineteen. I lived a double life, genuinely growing in love for the Lord Jesus but unable the change the homosexual desires I felt. I was utterly alone.

By the time I was nineteen I had become very good at hiding the pain I felt. I had been told by the media that I was born this way and that I should 'stop living a lie and 'embrace who I am'. I began to grieve the loss of ever being a husband or a father.

That was until I happened on a book called 'What some of you were.'[1] It is a collection of testimonies from men and women who have had their desires transformed by the power of the gospel. For the first time in years it seemed that there was hope for me, or at the very least that I hadn't been told the whole story. I had to find out more. I contacted recovery groups and they encouraged me to talk to a friend. Eventually I plucked up the courage to be honest with one friend, then another and another; every time experiencing the acceptance of God's people. I thank God for them because without them I would not have had the confidence to write this.

I have learned what it means to come into the light, to be exposed and vulnerable yet find yourself accepted and loved. Certainly, this is something every human being longs for, but perhaps those of us who are homosexual feel it more profoundly because of the rejection we perceive in society and sometimes (sadly) in the church.

As I write it has been six years since I first told someone about my homosexual desires and I would be lying if I said that it has been an easy road. I know what it is to wrestle with God; to beg, like Paul in 2 Corinthians 12, to have this 'thorn' taken away, yet find that it remains and conclude with him that Jesus' "grace is sufficient". Am I 'cured'? No. Yet I know that there is a transformation taking place.

I began this journey at the age of nineteen because I lamented the loss of a wife and children. I sought help because I desired 'recovery'. I wanted to be able to express myself sexually in a God-honouring way and raise children to know and love the Lord Jesus. Six years on I know that motivation was ill-placed. Let me be clear, I am not saying that marriage or sex is wrong, or that to desire fatherhood is wrong (in many ways those desires remain); but to allow them to become the *ultimate* longing of my heart is to pursue another false identity.

I am not defined by my homosexuality any more than my heterosexuality should define me if I am 'cured' overnight. I am a Christian; my identity is as one who has been washed (1 Corinthians 6:11), who as been adopted as a son (Romans 8:15) and who, with every other Christian, wrestles with the presence of sin until the redemption of our bodies in the new creation (Romans 8:23). This is what a it means to be truly human; to find our life, our hope, our joy in the one who assumed our humanity and by his redeeming death elevated it to the heights of his throne so that we might be able to sing those words in the hymn *Before the Throne of God Above*[2]:

> *One with himself I cannot die,*
> *My soul is purchased by his blood.*
> *My life is hid with Christ on high,*
> *With Christ my Saviour and my God.*

Does this mean that the struggle and temptations are gone? No, of course not. What it *does* mean is that I try to view them everyday, in the light of eternity.

I think one of the hardest things for us to begin to understand is that neither sex nor marriage are *rights* to be enjoyed, but gracious gifts from God. Does this mean that those who don't receive those gifts are any less 'human' or 'complete'? No, because whether we are married or single we are created in God's image and (as we have seen) true 'complete-ness' comes from having that image restored through forgiveness of sin and being transformed day by day into the likeness of Christ, who never married, never had sex yet was the most complete human being who ever lived.

There is so much more that could be said but allow me to make one final pastoral observation. It is easy to say to a Christian struggling with homosexuality, 'wait until heaven, it will be better then' or 'Jesus is more satisfying.' But honestly, those words often ring hollow. Theologically this truth is correct and wonderful but experientially it needs to be joined with the Church's desire to embrace and love homosexual Christians now, calling them to repentance and faith (just like everyone else) and encouraging them to live lives which honour and glorify God.

I have been very fortunate in that there have been many Christian brothers and sisters who have shown the love of Christ to me in allowing me into their lives. To know them and be fully known *by* them in a way that is not superficial but satisfying, not treating me as their 'project' to fix but as a member of their family. These are the relationships that will endure to the new creation, where there will be no marriage but one: the marriage of the Lamb and his bride, the Church.

[1] Christopher Keane (ed.) *What some of you were. Stories about Christians and homosexuality*', (Liberty Christian Ministries, 2001).
[2] Words: Charitie de Cheney Lees Smith Bancroft, 1863

Appendices

Further Reading

Gordon D. Fee, Douglas Smith, *How to Read the Bible for All its Worth*. (Grand Rapids: Zondervan, 2003)

Robert Gagnon, *The Bible and Homosexual Practice: Texts and Hermeneutics*. (Nashville: Abingdon Press, 2001)

A Goddard, G Harrison, *Unwanted Same-Sex Attraction – Issues of pastoral counselling and support*, (Christian Medical Fellowship 2011)

Wesley Hill, *Washed and Waiting*. (Grand Rapids, Michigan: Zondervan, 2010)

David Jackman, *Opening up the Bible*. (Bletchley, England: Scripture Union, 2006)

Stanton L. Jones and Mark A. Yarhouse, *Homosexuality: The Use of Scientific Research in the Church's Moral Debate*. (Downers Grove, Ill: InterVarsity Press, 2000)

S Jones & M Yarhouse, *Ex Gays? An Extended Longitudinal Study of Attempted Religiously Mediated Change in Sexual Orientation*, (IVP Academic)

Christopher Keane (ed.), *What some of you were. Stories about Christians and homosexuality*. (Liberty Christian Ministries, 2001)

David Peterson (ed.) *Holiness & Sexuality*. (Paternoster: Milton Keynes, UK and Waynesboro, GA, 2004)

Jeffrey Satinover, *Homosexuality and the Politics of Truth*. (Grand Rapids, MI: Baker, 1996)

John Stott, *Understanding the Bible*, (Reading: Scripture Union, 1984)
John Stott, 'Homosexual Partnerships?' in *Issues Facing Christians Today*. (London: Marshall Pickering, 1990)

The Christian Institute, *'Gay Marriage' in all but name*. (The Christian Institute, 2004)

Alex Tylee *Walking with Gay Friends. A journey of informed compassion* (Leicester: IVP, 2010)

Timothy Ward, *Words of Life: Scripture as the Living and Active Word of God.* (Nottingham: Inter-Varsity Press, 2009)

William J. Webb, *Slaves, Women & Homosexuals.* (Downers Grove, Ill: InterVarsity Press, 2001)

The Kuala Lumpur Statement

Statement on Human Sexuality
(2nd Anglican Encounter in the South, February 1997)

God's glory and loving purposes have been revealed in the creation of humankind (Rom. 1:18; Gen. 1:36, 27). Among the multiplicity of his gifts we are blessed with our sexuality.

1. Since the Fall (Gen. 3), life has been impaired and God's purposes spoilt. Our fallen state has affected every sphere of our being, which includes our sexuality. Sexual deviation has existed in every time and in most cultures. Jesus' teaching about lust in the Sermon on the Mount (Matt. 5:27-30) makes it clear that sexual sin is a real danger and temptation to us all.

2. It is, therefore, with an awareness of our own vulnerability to sexual sin that we express our profound concern about recent developments relating to Church discipline and moral teaching in some provinces in the North - specifically, the ordination of practicing homosexuals and the blessing of same-sex unions.

3. While acknowledging the complexities of our sexual nature and the strong drives it places within us, we are quite clear about God's will in this area which is expressed in the Bible.

4. The Scripture bears witness to God's will regarding human sexuality which is to be expressed only within the life long union of a man and a woman in (holy) matrimony.

5. The Holy Scriptures are clear in teaching that all sexual promiscuity is sin. We are convinced that this includes homosexual practices between men or women, as well as heterosexual relationships outside marriage.

6. We believe that the clear and unambiguous teaching of the Holy Scriptures about human sexuality is of great help to Christians as it provides clear boundaries.

7. We find no conflict between clear biblical teaching and sensitive pastoral care. Repentance precedes forgiveness and is part of the healing process. To heal spiritual wounds in God's name we need his wisdom and truth. We see this in the ministry of Jesus, for example his response to the adulterous women, "...neither do I condemn you. Go and sin no more." (John 8:11)

8. We encourage the Church to care for all those who are trapped in their sexual brokenness and to become the channel of Christ's compassion and love towards them. We wish to stand alongside and welcome them into a process of being whole and restored within our communities of faith. We would also affirm and resource those who exercise a pastoral ministry in this area.

9. We are deeply concerned that the setting aside of biblical teaching in such actions as the ordination of practicing homosexuals and the blessing of same-sex unions calls into question the authority of the Holy Scriptures. This is totally unacceptable to us.

10. This leads us to express concern about mutual accountability and interdependence within our Anglican Communion. As provinces and dioceses, we need to learn how to seek each other's counsel and wisdom in a spirit of true unity, and to reach a common mind before embarking on radical changes to Church discipline and moral teaching.

11. We live in a global village and must be more aware that the way we act in one part of the world can radically affect the mission and witness of the Church in another.

The Lambeth Conference 1998 Resolution I.10

Human Sexuality

This Conference:

a. commends to the Church the subsection report on human sexuality;

b. in view of the teaching of Scripture, upholds faithfulness in marriage between a man and a woman in lifelong union, and believes that abstinence is right for those who are not called to marriage;

c. recognises that there are among us persons who experience themselves as having a homosexual orientation. Many of these are members of the Church and are seeking the pastoral care, moral direction of the Church, and God's transforming power for the living of their lives and the ordering of relationships. We commit ourselves to listen to the experience of homosexual persons and we wish to assure them that they are loved by God and that all baptised, believing and faithful persons, regardless of sexual orientation, are full members of the Body of Christ;

d. while rejecting homosexual practice as incompatible with Scripture, calls on all our people to minister pastorally and sensitively to all irrespective of sexual orientation and to condemn irrational fear of homosexuals, violence within marriage and any trivialisation and commercialisation of sex;

e. cannot advise the legitimising or blessing of same sex unions nor ordaining those involved in same gender unions;

f. requests the Primates and the ACC to establish a means of monitoring the work done on the subject of human sexuality in the Communion and to share statements and resources among us;

g. notes the significance of the Kuala Lumpur Statement on Human Sexuality and the concerns expressed in resolutions IV.26, V.1, V.10, V.23 and V.35 on the authority of Scripture in matters of marriage and sexuality and asks the Primates and the ACC to include them in their monitoring process.

The Jerusalem Declaration

The Jerusalem Declaration was made at the GAFCON (Global Anglican Future Conference) held in Jerusalem in 2008.

In the name of God the Father, God the Son and God the Holy Spirit:

We, the participants in the Global Anglican Future Conference, have met in the land of Jesus' birth. We express our loyalty as disciples to the King of kings, the Lord Jesus. We joyfully embrace his command to proclaim the reality of his kingdom which he first announced in this land. The gospel of the kingdom is the good news of salvation, liberation and transformation for all. In light of the above, we agree to chart a way forward together that promotes and protects the biblical gospel and mission to the world, solemnly declaring the following tenets of orthodoxy which underpin our Anglican identity.

1. We rejoice in the gospel of God through which we have been saved by grace through faith in Jesus Christ by the power of the Holy Spirit. Because God first loved us, we love him and as believers bring forth fruits of love, ongoing repentance, lively hope and thanksgiving to God in all things.

2. We believe the Holy Scriptures of the Old and New Testaments to be the Word of God written and to contain all things necessary for salvation. The Bible is to be translated, read, preached, taught and obeyed in its plain and canonical sense, respectful of the church's historic and consensual reading.

3. We uphold the four Ecumenical Councils and the three historic Creeds as expressing the rule of faith of the one holy catholic and apostolic Church.

4. We uphold the Thirty-nine Articles as containing the true doctrine of the Church agreeing with God's Word and as authoritative for Anglicans today.

5. We gladly proclaim and submit to the unique and universal Lordship of Jesus Christ, the Son of God, humanity's only Saviour from sin, judgement and hell, who lived the life we could not live and died the death that we deserve. By his atoning death and glorious resurrection, he secured the redemption of all who come to him in repentance and faith.

6. We rejoice in our Anglican sacramental and liturgical heritage as an expression of the gospel, and we uphold the 1662 Book of Common Prayer as a true and authoritative standard of worship and prayer, to be translated and locally adapted for each culture.

7. We recognise that God has called and gifted bishops, priests and deacons in historic succession to equip all the people of God for their ministry in the world. We uphold the classic Anglican Ordinal as an authoritative standard of clerical orders.

8. We acknowledge God's creation of humankind as male and female and the unchangeable standard of Christian marriage between one man and one woman as the proper place for sexual intimacy and the basis of the family. We repent of our failures to maintain this standard and call for a renewed commitment to lifelong fidelity in marriage and abstinence for those who are not married.

9. We gladly accept the Great Commission of the risen Lord to make disciples of all nations, to seek those who do not know Christ and to baptise, teach and bring new believers to maturity.

10. We are mindful of our responsibility to be good stewards of God's creation, to uphold and advocate justice in society, and to seek relief and empowerment of the poor and needy.

11. We are committed to the unity of all those who know and love Christ and to building authentic ecumenical relationships.

We recognise the orders and jurisdiction of those Anglicans who uphold orthodox faith and practice, and we encourage them to join us in this declaration.

12. We celebrate the God-given diversity among us which enriches our global fellowship, and we acknowledge freedom in secondary matters. We pledge to work together to seek the mind of Christ on issues that divide us.

13. We reject the authority of those churches and leaders who have denied the orthodox faith in word or deed. We pray for them and call on them to repent and return to the Lord.

14. We rejoice at the prospect of Jesus' coming again in glory, and while we await this final event of history, we praise him for the way he builds up his church through his Spirit by miraculously changing lives.

#0070 - 020318 - C0 - 234/156/5 - PB - DID2138821